Praise For Everyting You 1
about Abortion – Fc

"Janet Morana's book *Everything You Need to Know About Abortion – For Teens* is a compelling personal journey of how Christ touched her heart to become the pro-life warrior she is today. This book is a must read for all those who even question the thought that 'abortion is the answer to all my problems.' Hearts will be transformed reading this excellent book."

—Sr. Deirdre (Dede) Byrne, POSC, Little Workers of the Sacred Hearts

"I applaud the focus of Janet Morana's book, *Everything You Need to Know About Abortion – For Teens*. Her no-nonsense approach directed toward teens addresses a critical need for today and for the future. It is a reminder that every life is precious. We mourn the loss of the aborted children but we also need to remember that today's teens are survivors in a culture of death. Although they survived to be born into this world, they often find themselves in empty lives. I believe Janet's book will help them to not only learn why abortion is evil but to also learn that they are always precious in the sight of God. Let us pray that Ms. Morana's work will impact the value of every life in wondrous ways."

—Bishop Joseph E. Strickland, Diocese of Tyler, Texas

"The abortion industry preys on vulnerable teens, establishing a dangerous relationship that normalizes risky sexual behavior and offers abortion violence when this inevitably leads to pregnancy. It is the prerogative of all concerned Americans to put a stop to this abuse. Standing between Big

Abortion and the nation's youth has been a primary objective of Students for Life of America for over fifteen years. I am incredibly grateful for Janet Morana's stalwart commitment to protecting American teens and their preborn children from abortion violence."

—Kristan Hawkins, President of Students for Life of America

"Whether you are a teen or a parent of a teen and you still have a scintilla of doubt that abortion is the intentional taking of an innocent human life, then you want to dive deep into this amazing pool of data, facts and science that is Janet Morana's gift to us."

—Joan Lewis, EWTN Rome Special Contributor and Host of "Joan's Rome" and "Vatican Insider"

"*Everything You Need to Know About Abortion – For Teens* has accomplished something crucial for the Church's ministry: It speaks directly to young people not only about abortion but about the many threats to their health and happiness that exist when they turn away from God and into the darkness of our culture. This is a message every young person needs to hear. Parish youth groups will find this to be a valuable resource!"

—Bishop Joseph L. Coffey, Archdiocese for the Military Services, USA

"There is an old saying that rings so very true when it comes to abortion: 'What you don't know can hurt you.' A vast majority of those who call themselves 'pro-choice' know so very little about this hot-button issue. Whether it is concerning the initial Supreme Court decision of Roe v. Wade which gave us abortion on demand through nine months of pregnancy, or the research that shows a majority of women don't actually 'choose' abortion but are instead pressured into one, too many know very little about the reality of abortion. That's why Janet Morana's latest book is a such a timely and valuable resource. Through not only the latest statistics and medical research but also through personal stories of those connected to abortion and the culture of death, this book further educates and affirms members of the pro-life community and provides a way to quietly witness to those who for whatever reason believe that abortion is still necessary."

—Teresa Tomeo, syndicated Catholic talk show host and best-selling Catholic author

"It is the young who most hear the siren-call of the secular society. It is they who are pulled into the widening chasm between moral realities and the group-think of popular culture. Their thinking and emotions are shaped by the media, entertainment, and their peers. But just as the young are more vulnerable to being misled, so too are they more open to being well led. Janet Morana walks teens through the moral and scientific nonsense that, like rickety stilts, supports the abortion industry. By giving them facts and appealing to basic human reason, and by sharing so many personal stories from her decades spent in the pro-life movement, she will no doubt influence the next generation of those ready to become pro-lifers."

—Dr. Ray Guarendi, host of EWTN's "Living Right with Dr. Ray"

EVERYTHING YOU NEED TO KNOW ABOUT ABORTION

—

FOR TEENS

JANET MORANA

TAN Books
Gastonia, North Carolina

Unless otherwise noted, Scripture quotations are from the Revised Standard Version of the Bible—Second Catholic Edition (Ignatius Edition), copyright © 2006 National Council of the Churches of Christ in the United States of America. Used by permission. All rights reserved.

Cover design by Andrew Schmalen.

Cover image: Sad man silhouette worried on the beach, by Antonioguillem/Adobe Stock. Couple silhouette breaking up a relation, by Antonioguillem/Adobe Stock.

Library of Congress Control Number: 2022931295

ISBN: 978-1-5051-2237-4
Kindle ISBN: 978-1-5051-2238-1
ePUB ISBN: 978-1-5051-2239-8

Published in the United States by
TAN Books
PO Box 269
Gastonia, NC 28053
www.TANBooks.com

Printed in the United States of America

Contents

Foreword

If you have picked up this book, you know that it is about the heated topic of abortion. You may have a personal interest in the subject, or maybe someone gave it to you to read. Or maybe you consider yourself pro-choice but are rethinking your position.

Whatever the reason, it is a good thing to ask yourself these questions: What do I really know about abortion, and why should I care about it? Is it really a choice for women, and if so, what are women (and men) choosing?

Before you make any decision, it is important to know all the facts. Reading this book will give you all the information you need to know about abortion, including scientific studies and documentation, personal stories, and other timely resources. Some of it will be disturbing and even shocking. Some of it will be heartbreaking. But you will see why this is still such a hot-button issue after abortion was legalized in the United States in 1973.

Did you know that one-third of your generation is missing because of abortion? Do you know that women have been lied to and manipulated for the past fifty years on the back of a billion-dollar business?

In this book, you will learn about the history and the deep, dark secrets of the abortion industry and why many of those involved in promoting it have since changed their minds. Only then can you make your own choice, because you will have all the facts, many of which continue to be hidden. You will also learn about the help that is available to women who may have made this decision and are still suffering in silence. I can assure you, healing is possible for anyone who desires it.

How do I know all this, and why should you believe me? To begin answering that, I should tell you that I have worked with college students in campus ministry for the last fifteen years at a large state university in New Jersey. The college campus is where many students get involved in sexual rela-tionships, often for the first time. Most colleges encourage sexual behavior as a rite of passage and part of the college experience, as long as it is consensual and safe. But what exactly does that mean?

I have listened to many stories of regret and pain and even counseled those seeking abortion. Often I was successful, but sometimes I was not. You see, I have a personal experi-ence of having an abortion as a teenager. I know what it's like to be a junior in high school with an unplanned pregnancy. I know what it's like to be in fear of your parents and ashamed of how this even happened in the first place. I know what it's like to experience the pain and suffering of having to face this tragedy alone as a young girl. I also know what it's like to be in denial of the pain of abortion for twenty-five years. I share this with you so that you will be aware of all of the untold secrets as to why abortion hurts women, men, fami-lies, and all of the children lost to it. I believe knowledge is power, and my goal is to try to speak truth in love and give others as much information as possible.

Sadly, this didn't happen for me. I had no idea what I was getting into when I was told abortion would be the only solution for me. At sixteen, I was on top of the world. I was a junior in a great high school. I had many friends and was an accomplished student who loved art and music. Things got even better when I met my first boyfriend. He was gentle, compassionate, and from a wonderful family. I thought my life was complete. Things changed when, after some time, he encouraged me to become sexually active. He claimed this would cement our relationship. I thought I was so in love that all I wanted to do was to please him. It was the height of what was called the *sexual revolution*, a social movement that began in the 1960s. It challenged traditional roles of sexual behavior and separated sex from marriage and the creation of life.

I made the decision to abandon my fears and trusted the promises offered from the culture that embraced this *new* commandment of love. This love was free, without boundaries or consequences. It was free from commitment. This love was all about feelings and desire. It didn't matter if one person got hurt. I was told there would be no regrets. There would be no emotional fallout. This love was only meant to feel good, but in essence, this new so-called love declared war on what love was really supposed to be. It was only the beginning of the lies. My deep desire to be loved, especially after not receiving love from my own father, made it easy to believe in the false promises of my generation. I surrendered willingly to this distorted love, unprepared for the battleground it would leave in my heart.

Six months into our relationship, I learned I was pregnant. I had just turned seventeen in early May of 1972. When the news was confirmed by a doctor at Planned Parenthood, I was overwhelmed with fear in a way I had never felt before. It was a fear that threatened my security on the highest levels. It was a fear I had not planned or been prepared for. This fear took over my body and my soul. I feared what my parents would say, especially my father. I had fear of being kicked out of my Catholic school (which at the time would have happened). I had a fear of telling my boyfriend (who had already left me) and what my community would think. Yet, as hard as it was trying to deal with this overwhelming amount of fear, I was also grieving the loss of my virginity and the loss of my child. Had this all been worth it?

Fear had led me to the belief in the lies surrounding abortion. No one would ever find out. After all, the doctor at Planned Parenthood told me it was just a clump of cells and tissue even though I was eleven weeks pregnant. She promised I would be able to go on with my life as if nothing had happened. But just the opposite came true. Lies were exposed as I left the abortion clinic on that day, August 1, 1972. It was before *Roe v. Wade*, the January 22, 1973 Supreme Court decision that legalized abortion across the country. Abortion was only legal in a few states when I discovered I was pregnant. New York was one of them. The clinic I was sent to was called CRASH, The Center for Reproductive and Sexual Health, owned and operated by the well-known abortion doctor the late Bernard Nathanson. This "abortion king" operated the largest abortion clinic, located in New York City. You will hear more about him later in this book.

Following the procedure, I was deeply traumatized as fear turned into guilt and shame. It was not a simple surgical procedure as I had been promised. I knew I would have to stuff my grief way down as a way of trying to cope with all the loss and confusion. The doctor and nurses had no concern for my welfare that day. I was just a number to push the need for this to be legal. When it was over, I was given a pack of birth control pills and an antibiotic and sent on my way. It was all about the money.

After an abortion, the body remembers, because the womb is the heart of the woman, a sacred place where any assault leaves lasting damage. I had to detach my mind, my heart, and my emotions. In shutting these off, my heart hardened and turned cold. Initially, there is a relief of not having to face uncertainty, but that often turns to great sadness. I became angry and resentful to all those around me. I had a deep shame and a profound sense of loss. Now I was terribly fearful of my secret ever being revealed. So what do you do with all this unresolved grief? You stuff it down deep, somewhere, anywhere, and do everything you can to numb it and hope it goes away.

I have come to believe that many women who have had abortions have bought into this type of existence, as I tried to do. I'm good. I'll get over it. Dealing with the truth is too hard. Statistics show the majority of women didn't have a choice; they were coerced by a father, a mother, or a boyfriend. Often, you will hear women saying it was *her* body, so it was *her* choice. It sounds logical, but science tells us something different. There are two bodies and two hearts beating (or more if there are multiple babies). A woman's body is the *place* where the baby inside her grows, from the moment of conception. Again, these are scientific facts, not opinions. You might hear a woman shout that her abortion empowered her and helped her to get to where she is today. She has no regrets. These are lies used to assuage a guilty conscience, whether she knows it or not.

Many of us who have had abortions have come to learn in our own journeys, often the hard way, that denial is often our first friend. Denial helps you to deal with the devastation, so you continue to push it down and move forward. But denial can bring darkness. Women and men who have come forward in telling their stories have experienced similar struggles with alcohol, drugs, promiscuity, broken relationships, and often, more abortions. In addition to the emotional pain, there are many physical consequences, including depression, anxiety, infertility, and even cancer. But I am not here to judge anyone and force those who do not desire healing. I am only here to share my own personal story and to be a voice for those who do not have one or who are in fear of speaking out about their own abortions.

It was twenty-five years later, after the birth of my only living child, that I began my healing process. I attended a Rachel's Vineyard retreat, developed by Dr. Theresa Burke, on the anniversary of *Roe v. Wade* in 1999, with six other women and one man. It was a weekend that changed my life. In time, I learned to fully accept the responsibility for my actions as well as the consequences that have come into my life as a result of my choice. I also found that I was not alone. As my healing progressed, I began to make amends with my family, my parents, and my siblings and extended family and friends, all those who were affected by my abortion and behavior. Abortion harms a lot more people besides the mother, the father, and the child. But there is hope, healing, and restoration. One of my most important opportunities was to be able to attend the funeral of Dr. Nathanson, the abortion doctor who had his own change of heart later in life, as did the late Norma McCorvey (the Jane Roe in the court case). These stories are important.

I will continue to speak out about my own experience, especially if it can change the heart and mind of even one person. I am a proud member of the Silent No More Awareness Campaign, co-founded by Georgette Forney and my dear friend Janet Morana. I thank Janet for writing this important book for young people during such an important time as this. Share the truth, and always do it with compassion and love!

Mary Kominsky
St. John Henry Newman Catholic Center,
Montclair (NJ) State University

My Way or God's Way

Human Life vs. Animal Life

You might have strong opinions about abortion. You might even consider yourself pro-choice. But there are times when life's circumstances can provide a different twist to your thinking

When I was an early childhood public school teacher in New York City, most of my colleagues considered themselves pro-choice. My good friend and team teacher Denise would adamantly proclaim herself to be pro-choice, while I was the token pro-lifer in our school.

One spring semester, we decided to hatch chickens in our classroom. We ordered all the appropriate equipment, including our precious fertilized chick eggs. The children were so excited to watch nature at its best right before their eyes.

One morning, when we entered the classroom, Denise and I noticed a problem with one of the eggs. The shell was cracked open and we could see a yellow yolk sac and a bloody mass pulsing like a beating heart. In fact, it was the beating heart of a chick that was not going to develop further. Denise and I were both upset, not knowing what to do. Denise gasped, "It's still alive!" I knew that but also knew there was nothing we could do to save it. Within moments, the chick's heart stopped beating. Denise was very upset at the loss of this chick in the very early stages of development.

So how could Denise be pro-choice on abortion? She was obviously a very sensitive person, but when it came to abortion, logic seemed to vanish. Many people who consider themselves pro-choice think it is perfectly fine to terminate the life of an unborn child in the first trimester. So why is it when it comes to animals, people are suddenly more pro-life than ever before?

Let's talk about dogs. One dog is pregnant with a litter of six pedigree puppies, while a mixed breed is also pregnant with a litter of six. The owner of the pedigree will have no problem selling those six puppies, making a decent profit, while the owner of the mixed breed will probably have a difficult time finding homes for the puppies. So why not abort the mixed-breed puppies? After all, don't we have enough stray dogs wandering the streets already? Well, you can bet that if you aborted puppies, there would be a public outcry, and I am sure the media would cover the story.

So why is it that when we talk about the destruction of human lives from abortion, our conversation is couched in terms like "a woman's right to choose," or "reproductive health," but with puppies, there is an almost unanimous pro-life opinion?

The Nature of Choice

Let's now consider the term *pro-choice*. It sounds very good; in fact, it is very American to be in favor of freedom of choice. But there are certain times when your freedom of choice must be limited because your choice infringes upon the rights of another person. For example, I do not have the "freedom of choice" to smash your car, steal from a store, or assault another human being.

Yet when it comes to abortion, we couch the killing of an unborn child as a woman's right to choose. Yes, you have the right to choose many things, like what foods you want to eat, the type of car you want to drive, the college you want to attend. But why do we use the *pro-choice* term so loosely when it comes to abortion? I think many people use that slogan without thinking deeply about the consequences of it.

The more accurate term here would be *pro-abortion*. And yet there are many Americans who really aren't paying attention at all to the abortion issue. They have no idea what the Supreme Court decision *Roe v. Wade* was about, and in fact the abortion issue isn't even on their radar screen. That really sums up where I was at one time.

While I never considered myself pro-choice, I also wouldn't have labeled myself pro-life. The truth is, I never gave abortion a second thought growing up in the 1960s and 1970s.

So what about you? Maybe you are being raised in a very pro-life family, or maybe your family members identify as "pro-choice." Either way, it's time for you to at least be open to learning some facts about this issue. Let me tell you a little about myself and why I would like you to read this book and to keep an open mind.

My Own Journey

I was born in Brooklyn, New York, in 1952 and was educated in Catholic schools. I am the oldest of four children, with fourteen years separating me from my youngest sibling. My study of religion was from the Baltimore Catechism, which was a question-and-answer format.

Spiritual direction was something that just didn't exist for the average layperson. We memorized all our prayers. My family didn't even have a Bible in the house. But on Sunday morning, we all went to Mass. Church was a place of warmth, comfort, and stability. In fact, when meeting new people, we commonly identified ourselves by the name of our parish—mine was Saint Vincent Ferrer, in the Flatbush section of Brooklyn. I would say, "I'm from Saint Vinny's!"

I attended an all-girl, small Catholic high school, Saint Agnes Seminary in Brooklyn, staffed by the Sisters of Saint Joseph. During my sophomore year, the Church went through a radical change. On July 25, 1968, Pope Paul VI issued an encyclical called *Humanae Vitae*. He was expected to drop the Church's ban on artificial contraception, but he did just the opposite. He *reaffirmed* it, ushering in a new division in the Church. You could literally go to a priest on one side of a church and be told that birth control was a sin, while on the other side of the same church another priest would say it wasn't a sin, so long as you had a "good reason" to avoid pregnancy. Let's face it, we can all justify our behavior if we really want to and try hard enough. The culture, too, was changing. I bet if you're Catholic, you rarely hear your priests preach about contraception being a sin.

When I was a teenager, the sexual revolution, "women's lib," and the whole drug culture were in full swing. I have to confess, I got caught up in this whole changing world. I began to question my faith. I thought women had a right to birth control, and I no longer believed in the infallibility of the pope. All those Baltimore Catechism questions and answers became irrelevant.

How do you feel about the Church you are attending? Do you go to Mass because you really want to go, or are you going because your parents expect you to go? There is a defining moment when many teens make a conscious decision to stop going to Mass. That's the first step down a slippery slope.

Here's how my journey away from the Church began.

It was my sophomore year at Saint Agnes, and the priest came to our school for our monthly confession. I dutifully lined up with my class. This time, though, I began to feel anxious and no longer wanted to make my confession. I did an about-face and walked back into class. Sister asked, "Did you make your confession, Janet?" and I replied, "Yes, Sister." So began my first steps away from the Church that had nurtured me. I stopped going to confession, which led me to abstain from Communion, which in turn led to me skipping Mass altogether. In the end, I only attended Mass on Christmas and Easter.

Fast forward a little. I graduated from Saint Francis College in 1974 and got married in 1975. It was a time when my Catholic faith no longer seemed to matter to me. My relationship with God was almost at a zero. At the same time, all my close friends were getting married, so marriage seemed like the next step to take, or so I thought.

I became engaged after dating my future husband for just three months. From there, things moved quickly towards our wedding day. At pre-cana classes, the priest told us that depending upon the circumstances, birth control pills could be an option for us to consider. I didn't realize at the time that this was bad advice in every way—theologically, spiritually, psychologically, and physically!

As the oldest of four siblings, I had many years of experience dealing with diapers and babysitting and felt that delaying the start of a family was a good idea. I had taken birth control pills back in high school (although I wasn't sexually active), as prescribed by my Catholic OB/GYN for menstrual problems. At this point in my life, then, both a priest and a doctor had legitimized the use of contraceptives, and so I continued my journey down that slippery slope.

I started taking birth control pills three months before my wedding date. About one month before our wedding, my fiancé began to pressure me sexually. I was a virgin but gave in to the pressure, and so my marriage got off to a bad start.

When you begin marriage not knowing each other very well and then compound things by moving into a very intimate physical relationship, you set the stage for disaster. There's a popular song about marrying your best friend; well, that's how well you should know someone before entering into such a serious, lifelong commitment. But that's 20-20 hindsight advice from me. And of course, you shouldn't have sex before marriage. Please don't roll your eyes right now; stick with me, because in future chapters, I will show you just the facts as to why having many sexual partners before settling on someone to marry can be very damaging to you physically, psychologically, and yes, spiritually, but we will delve into that later in this book.

Now back to my story! I continued taking the pill for two years. Once I stopped, I got pregnant and gave birth to an absolutely beautiful baby girl, Jennifer. I threw all my attention into motherhood, and as a result, wanted to delay having another baby. I went back on birth control until my daughter was thirteen months old. Then I felt it was important for her to have a sibling, so I stopped taking the pill. Once again, I became pregnant almost immediately. These experiences gave me the false impression that the pill was "working"; I was in control of planning my family. Me. Not God.

This time, I gave birth to beautiful twin girls, Tara and Kelly. By this time, birth control pills were being linked with an increased risk of blood clots and strokes. With a history of strokes in my family, I was afraid to start taking them again. I didn't know about Natural Family Planning.[1] In fact, the only natural method I knew of was the old "rhythm" method, which was considered by most to be unreliable. Since my marriage was built on a physical relationship, you can imagine the amount of arguing and fighting that began.

---

[1]   Natural Family Planning (or "fertility awareness") is a method of contraception where a woman monitors and records different fertility signals during her menstrual cycle to work out when she's likely to get pregnant.

When the twins were three, I thought I was pregnant again. It was just "a scare," but it was enough to make me do something drastic: I had a procedure known as a tubal ligation that made it impossible for me to ever get pregnant again. I felt I had solved all my problems. I was wrong.

I had embraced everything the feminist movement promoted as being liberating and empowering for women. In reality, I had not been liberated; every day I felt more trapped in a bad marriage.

As my marriage continued its downward spiral, I focused more and more on my three daughters. The good news is that I became reconnected with my Catholic faith around this time. It was amazing how the hand of God worked. I was trying to get a job teaching in the public schools on Staten Island, but they were experiencing budget cuts and were not hiring. My mother-in-law, who was a daily communicant and also the person who took my daughters to Mass every Sunday for me, began praying a novena that I would find a job. I just rolled my eyes, being the "Doubting Thomasina" that I was. But then a Christmas miracle happened in 1988: I was hired to teach first grade at P.S. 31 on Staten Island.

My mother-in-law instructed me to go to church to light a candle of thanksgiving. Well, since it was Christmas and I at least went to Mass then, I went and lit my candle. I then went to Mass again the following Sunday, not wanting to chance anything happening to me as I started my new teaching position.

By the third week of attending Mass, the hand of God reached out for me again. We were leaving Saint Charles

Church when my daughter Tara called out to the newly ordained Father Frank Pavone to come over and meet her mom. She said, "Father Frank, here's my mom. You know, the one who needs to go to confession!"

I turned beet red. But Father Pavone was very measured and calmed down Tara's excitement. He turned to me and told me I didn't have to go to confession. Well, that was a relief! But he did give me the rectory phone number and told me to give him a call. He said we could just talk. Just talk about the Church? That seemed odd to me. So I stuffed the paper with his number in my pocketbook and there it stayed for a few more weeks.

Then one day, I stumbled across it again and decided to give this young priest a call. He invited me to his Friday night Bible study and we had an appointment after that for what I later found out was called spiritual direction. I gave him my laundry list of disagreements with the Church's teaching, and he wasn't shocked. He invited me to continue to come and study, and I took him up on the challenge. It took me three months of discussion and study and finally I was ready for confession. After twenty years away from the Church, I rediscovered the wealth we have with our Faith. I received Communion that day, and for me, it was just like my First Holy Communion. I knew I was beginning a relationship with Jesus.

You see, that was the secret ingredient that I never had before, a relationship with Jesus. Maybe you have a great relationship with Jesus, and maybe you don't. It's time to stop and think again about why you go to Mass every Sunday or why you skip it altogether. Because of the relationship

I now have with Jesus, I never want to miss Mass. In fact, I look forward to it. I also talk to Jesus, just like I would my friends, which is something I never learned from all the Catholic schools I attended. I even pray and read the Bible every day, things I never did before. I am currently doing a program that gives Bible verses to read every day so that by the end of the year, I will have read the entire Bible!

As I continued to rediscover my faith and the teachings of the Church, I learned about God's beautiful plan for marriage, including Natural Family Planning. At the same time, I became aware of how birth control pills really worked.

I always thought birth control pills simply prevented fertilization. But I came to learn that the pill actually has its own built-in insurance system, employing several different methods of action in case one or more of the methods don't work. Besides trying to prevent fertilization, the pill also thickens the cervical mucus, which then acts as a barrier, preventing the sperm from getting to the egg. If both of these first two methods fail and ovulation and conception both occur, then the pill acts to prevent the fertilized egg (the newly conceived *human being*) from implanting itself onto the side wall of the uterus. The child is then aborted out of the body.

I didn't feel the impact of this newfound information until several years later. I was with a friend visiting the Epcot Center in Disney World, and we decided to visit the Wonder of Life exhibit. As I began to watch a beautiful video showing how life begins, I realized what taking birth control pills really meant: *the possibility of aborting new life.* In the years that I had been taking birth control pills, I had been very sexually active. I also knew that I was an extremely fertile woman. Given these facts, I have no doubt that I had successfully conceived new life many times but had never given these babies the chance to grow inside me. For the very first time in my life, I came to grips with the fact that I had not only shut myself off to life but had also destroyed an unknown number of children.

As I came out of that exhibit, there was a giant rushing water fountain nearby. I walked over to it and began to sob uncontrollably. I stayed there for quite some time, absorbed in my sudden feelings of grief and remorse. This was the very first time I became aware of the full impact of what I had done.

As I became more involved in pro-life work, I learned more about the damage that abortion does to women. I realized that many post-abortive women felt alone in their grief at first, and ashamed to express it, but later were able to experience mercy and healing. These women who had been through the healing process could therefore serve as a voice for other women still locked in the secret sin of abortion.

That is why I co-founded the Silent No More Awareness Campaign, an initiative that gives women a forum for publicly testifying to the negative impact that abortion has had on their lives. Because I never had an abortion, people began to question why I was involved in such a campaign. Here again, I had to come to grips with all the children I had lost because of birth control pills.

When working in post-abortion ministry, one might be tempted only to recognize the pain and grief that comes from an abortion. Yet I know in my heart that the loss I feel is just as real as if I had had an abortion. Moreover, I know I am not alone. In fact, many women come up to me when I am at conferences speaking about the Silent No More Awareness Campaign and share their grief from years of taking abortifacients.

I am now reaching out to the other women who I know share these feelings, and I have found time and time again that I am not the only woman with a testimony like this. I know we can help many families realize the damage birth control will do to their lives by getting the word out. I also want to reach out to others who feel the pain that I have described and tell them that they, too, can take the first steps towards healing.

And finally, it is my hope that others like me who turned their back on Jesus will realize the true wealth we have in the documents and teachings of the Church, and the power the Lord gives us to live those teachings. It is my hope that they see their purpose in life as described so succinctly in the Baltimore Catechism: "To know, love and serve Him on Earth so that we may be happy with Him in Heaven." We are called to know Jesus Christ as our Lord and Savior and also as our friend. We are called to have a personal relationship with Him. I nearly threw this all away and turned my face away from Him for almost twenty years. I will spend whatever time I have left here on earth singing His praises and hopefully, through my story, bring others back to the Lord and His Bride, the Church!

You can see why I am so passionate about the life issue. At one time, I was clueless, but once I discovered the truth, it was like an iron door closed behind me and I couldn't go back, nor did I want to.

So now I would like to take you on a journey, if you will let me. We will learn many facts about how abortion became legal in the United States, what abortion does to an unborn child, and what abortion does to the mothers, fathers, grandparents, and future siblings. Yes, we will learn how abortion has had an impact on families and in fact all of society.

So let's begin.

2

Contraception—Just the Facts

The Link between Abortion and Contraception

If you're wondering why I'm talking about contraception instead of abortion, it's because the two are very much linked. In fact, the abortion industry began by promoting contraception because it is well known that failed contraception leads to abortion.

This chapter will deal with the science of birth control rather than the morality. The morality discussion is actually a shorter one. Artificial birth control goes against the teachings of the Catholic Church, as does sex outside of marriage. You are not supposed to be using contraception because it's a sin. *End of discussion.*

If you need further convincing, let's look at the science and origins of the pill and the state of contraception today.

A Changing Culture

History has recorded the 1960s as the time when a huge cultural shift began to take place in America. It was the birth of the "sexual revolution"—when the culture encouraged men and women to separate sex from love and marriage and to do what "felt good." Studies have shown that between 1965 and 1975, the number of women who had sexual intercourse prior to marriage increased dramatically.[1] Behavior that had once been condemned became the norm.

I was a teenager during the social and political upheaval of the 1960s. I started high school in September 1966, and I can remember things changing radically, and fast. In women's fashions, dresses got shorter and necklines plunged lower. I distinctly remember TV shows and movies changing too. In the early 1960s, married couples on TV shows slept in separate beds. By the latter years of the decade, married couples were able to share a bed, but intimacy was not in the picture. By 1972, though, the title character in the show "Maude" had an abortion that was openly discussed, and shows that would seem very tame by today's standards—like "The Love Boat" and "Fantasy Island"—dealt with themes that very often included sex outside of marriage. Ask your grandparents about this, because I'm sure they have many stories to tell.

Real life was keeping up with TV in the early 1970s. Although contraception was only legal for married couples, that was about to change. In 1972, the US Supreme Court, in the case of *Eisenstadt v. Baird*, expanded the right of

---

[1]   Amyra Grossbard-Shechtman Heer; "The Impact of the Female Marriage Squeeze and the Contraceptive Revolution on Sex Roles and the Women's Liberation Movement in the United States, 1960 to 1975," *Journal of Marriage and the Family* 43, no. 1. (February 1981), pp. 49–65.

privacy to unmarried people and made contraceptives legally available throughout the country.[2]

The Baird in the case is Bill Baird, and I have been friends with him for many years, despite our disagreements—and in fact, he even agrees with me that contraception and abortion go hand-in-hand. He was happy to talk to me about it while I was writing my book *Recall Abortion: Ending the Abortion Industry's Exploitation of Women* several years ago.

It was his mission to make contraception and abortion available to poor women. After he saw a woman die following a self-administered abortion in 1963, he worked on the front lines to challenge anti-birth control laws in New York, New Jersey, and Massachusetts. He would also give out various forms of contraception, including the pill, until he was arrested. His arrest in front of 2,500 people at Boston University for giving a condom and contraceptive foam to an unmarried woman became the case that made it to the Supreme Court.

"My goal was to be arrested," he told me. "I arranged to give a condom and a package of contraceptive foam to a nineteen-year-old girl. Twenty cops rushed me and handcuffed me. I also had with me a receipt for $3.09—nine cents was the sales tax—from Zayres Department Store, a big chain in New England, for the Emko foam. I said that if I was being arrested, the attorney general for Massachusetts also should be arrested for collecting sales tax on an illegal item."

Baird was found guilty of a felony in October 1967 and faced up to ten years in prison. His conviction was upheld

---

2   Eisenstadt v. Baird, 405 US 438 (1972).

by the Massachusetts Supreme Court, and his first application to bring the case before the US Supreme Court was rejected. His second appeal was accepted, and on March 22, 1972, the Supreme Court ruled that an individual's right to privacy was more important than anything, and that contraception was to be made legal for everyone, married or unmarried. His case is considered by many to be the foundation on which *Roe v. Wade* was built. Bill and I agree on that.

The birth control pill also was born during this decade of big changes. The scientists who developed the pill were eager to prove they could master the amazingly complex female reproductive system. At the same time, popular culture was beginning to embrace the idea that big families were bad and that there was no reason to wait until marriage to have sex. The pharmaceutical companies understood that the pill would make them very rich. No one, however, seemed to be thinking that the pill might be bad for women's health, and in fact, more than sixty years later, those health risks are still being largely ignored. If you look through any teen magazine, you'll probably see advertisements for different kinds of contraception, but you'll have to squint to read the fine print that lists all the health risks of each product.

So why are they on the market in the first place? Good question. Let's go back and see how they first made their way onto the American market.

A Troubling Trial

On May 10, 1960, the federal Food and Drug Administration approved the use of a pill called Enovid, which was a drug developed by the pharmaceutical company G. D. Searle for treating women and girls who had problems with their periods. Searle scientists realized Enovid could be used as a contraceptive, but they needed to try it out on women first. Researcher Gregory Pincus and physician John Rock looked south to Puerto Rico, a very poor US territory with a big population, where contraceptives were not illegal. According to a 2003 film called *The Pill*, the test trials began in 1965.

Here's a transcript from a section of the film:

> Dr. Edris Rice-Wray, a faculty member of the Puerto Rico Medical School and medical director of the Puerto Rico Family Planning Association, was in charge of the trials. After a year of tests, Dr. Rice-Wray reported good news to Pincus. The pill was 100 percent effective when taken properly. She also informed him that 17 percent of the women in the study complained of nausea, dizziness, headaches, stomach pain, and vomiting. So serious and sustained were the reactions that Rice-Wray told Pincus that a 10-milligram dose of Enovid caused "too many side reactions to be generally acceptable."
>
> Rock and Pincus quickly dismissed Rice-Wray's conclusions. Their patients in Boston had experienced far fewer negative reactions, and they believed many of the complaints were psychosomatic (in their heads). The men also felt that problems such as bloating and nausea were minor compared to the contraceptive benefits of the drug. Although three women died while participating in the trials, no investigation

was conducted to see if the pill had caused the young women's deaths. Confident in the safety of the pill, Pincus and Rock took no action to assess the root cause of the side effects.

In later years, Pincus's team would be accused of deceit, colonialism, and the exploitation of poor women of color. The women had only been told that they were taking a drug that prevented pregnancy, not that this was a clinical trial, that the pill was experimental, or that there was a chance of potentially dangerous side effects.[3]

To this day, questions remain over whether Pincus and Rock, who were so eager to get their drug to the market, overlooked serious side effects from the high doses of the hormones estrogen and progestin. In fact, when I visited Puerto Rico in 2006 to speak to women's groups in several cities and towns around the island, people shared with me their personal knowledge of the drug trials. Many felt there had been a massive cover-up about the terrible effects experienced by the women who participated in this research without even knowing it.

Clearly, the Searle researchers held little regard for women's health. But things must be better now in this enlightened age of ours, right?

Hardly.

---

[3]   *The Pill*, written and directed by Chana Gazit, aired February 24, 2003, on PBS, https://www.pbs.org/wgbh/americanexperience/films/pill/#film_description.

Dangerous Side Effects

In addition to blood clots, the pill poses lots of other serious health risks to women, including increased risk of heart disease, cervical cancer, and, to a lesser extent with newer drugs, stroke.[4]

The main health risk question, however, is how the pill impacts a woman's risk of breast cancer.

The medical community agrees the risk of breast cancer is greater in women who have an increased exposure to the hormone estrogen. Birth control pills do just this—increasing a woman's exposure to estrogen. Therefore, the longer a woman takes the pill, the greater her risk of breast cancer. It seems the argument should end there, but because abortion is such a political and socially divisive issue (not to mention financially lucrative), and because contraception and abortion are blood relatives, so to speak, researchers tend to downplay or outright ignore the link between the pill and an increased risk of breast cancer.

---

[4]   "FDA Drug Safety Communication: Updated information about the FDA-funded study on risk of blood clots in women taking birth control pills containing drospirenone," U.S. Food & Drug Administration, updated October 2021, http://www.fda.gov/Dr ugs/DrugSafety/ucm277346.htm. Shufelt, Baire Merz, "Contraceptive Hormone Use and Cardiovascular Disease," *Journal of the American College of Cardiology*, January 20, 2009, http://content .onlinejacc.org/cgi/content/full/53/3/221?maxtoshow=&hits=10 &RESULTFORMAT=&fulltext=contraception+shufelt+mertz& searchid=1&FIRSTINDEX=0&resourcetype=HWCIT.   Caitlin Carlton, Matthew Banks, and Sophia Sundararajan, "Oral Contraceptives and Ischemic Stroke Risk," *American Heart Association* 49, no. 4 (March 16, 2018), https://www.ahajournals.org/doi/full /10.1161/STROKEAHA.117.020084.

Dr. Angela Lanfranchi, a New Jersey breast cancer surgeon who was in private practice for more than thirty years before retiring, said the increased cancer risk is often understated by both doctors and the media because, statistically, it is a small increase. "What they neglect to say is that a low risk in millions of women translates into tens of thousands of extra cases of cancer," Dr. Lanfranchi explains.[5] Breast cancer is the second most common kind of cancer in women, after skin cancer. More than forty-three thousand women in the United States die each year of breast cancer.[6]

In 1999, combined oral contraceptives (those that use both estrogen and progesterone) were identified as carcinogens in Group 1—that is, substances that cause cancer—by the International Agency for Research on Cancer, an arm of the World Health Organization. Following a 2005 review, the designation did not change.[7] It is still true today.

But cancer is not the only problem the pill causes for women or society in general. Dr. Lanfranchi points to studies showing that changing a woman's hormonal profile can cause her to choose the wrong partner for a husband, which could be a contributing factor in our society's high divorce rates. This sounds a little bit like science fiction, but it's true.

---

[5]   Angela Lanfranchi, interview with author.

[6]   "U.S. Breast Cancer Statistics," BreastCancer.org, modified February 2, 2021, https://www.breastcancer.org/symptoms/understand _bc/statistics.

[7]   "Carcinogenicity of combined hormonal contraceptives and combined menopausal treatment," World Health Organization, September 2005, http://www.who.int/reproductivehealth/topics/age ing/cocs_hrt_statement.pdf.

The *Wall Street Journal* reported on the scientific study that uncovered this phenomenon in May 2011:

> Much of the attraction between the sexes is chemistry. New studies suggest that when women use hormonal contraceptives, such as birth control pills, it disrupts some of these chemical signals, affecting their attractiveness to men and women's own preferences for romantic partners.
>
> The type of man a woman is drawn to is known to change during her monthly cycle—when a woman is fertile, for instance, she might look for a man with more masculine features. Taking the pill or another type of hormonal contraceptive upends this natural dynamic, making less-masculine men seem more attractive, according to a small but growing body of evidence. The findings have led researchers to wonder about the implications for partner choice, relationship quality and even the health of the children produced by these partnerships.[8]

---

[8]   Shirley S. Wang, "The Tricky Chemistry of Attraction," *The Wall Street* Journal, May 9, 2011, http://online.wsj.com/article/SB10 0014240527487046819045763132435796773316.html. See also Alexandra Alvergne and Virpi Lummaa, "Does the Contraceptive Pill Alter Mate Choice in Humans," *Trends in Ecology & Evolution*, March 2010, http://www.sciencedirect.com/science/article/pii/S0 169534709002638.

Beyond the Pill

Birth control options are no longer confined to just the pill. There are birth-control patches, vaginal rings, implants, and shots to choose from. All of them are bad medicine with potentially deadly or life-altering side effects. You don't have to take my word for it. The Mayo Clinic is a well-respected medical center and research facility with its main headquarters in Minnesota. If you want to know the truth about a drug, you can find it by doing a search at MayoClinic.org. What you'll find about the various birth-control methods is truly eye-opening.

Let's start with the patch. There are two varieties—Twirla and Xulane.

Twirla is a patch that women place on their upper torso, buttocks, or back. It must be changed every week for three weeks; no patch is worn during the fourth week to allow for a menstrual period.

About Twirla, the Mayo Clinic website notes it is less effective in women and girls whose body mass index (BMI) is between 25 and 30 and can cause serious heart complications and increased risk for blood clots for those with BMI over 30. Cigarette smokers are warned against using Twirla because the risk of blood clots, heart attacks, and strokes is increased. It can cause gall bladder problems and liver disease. It also can affect your mood.

According to the Mayo Clinic: "This medicine may cause some people to be agitated, irritable, or display other abnormal behaviors, such as feeling sad or hopeless, getting upset easily, or feeling nervous or hostile. It may also cause some people to become more depressed."[9]

Until Twirla came along, Xulane (also known as Ortho Evra) was the only birth-control patch on the market. It's another bad drug with virtually the same list of possible side effects and warnings, except it contains more estrogen than Twirla, meaning the risk of being diagnosed with breast cancer is higher.

The Mayo Clinic provides a long list of drugs that should not be taken together with Xulane. It also makes users more susceptible to serious sunburn, something you might not discover until it is too late.

If you don't like the idea of changing a patch every week, a doctor might suggest an implant. Nexplanon is a plastic rod about the size of a matchstick that is implanted in the upper arm. It's very effective at preventing pregnancy for up to three years but can be removed at any time. Women who do get pregnant with Nexplanon are at an increased risk for an ectopic pregnancy—a baby growing outside the womb—which can cause infertility and even death. It comes with the same laundry list of side effects as the patch, including blood clots, heart attack, stroke, ovarian cysts, and more.[10] Smokers should not use the implant.

---

[9]   "Levonorgestrel And Ethinyl Estradiol (Transdermal Route)," Mayo Clinic, last updated November 1, 2021, https://www.mayo clinic.org/drugs-supplements/levonorgestrel-and-ethinyl-estra diol-transdermal-route/precautions/drg-20484134.

[10]   "Side Effects of NEXPLANON," Organon, accessed November 15, 2021, https://www.nexplanon.com/side-effects/.

A device called a vaginal ring is sold under the brand name NuvaRing. Women insert the ring themselves and leave it in for three weeks every month. NuvaRing has proven deadly for more than forty women, and hundreds of lawsuits have been filed against Merck, the drug company that makes it. Why it is still on the market—now along with a number of competitors, like Estring and Femring—is a perfect example of how profit is much more important than women's health. In December 2020, it was predicted by Grand View Research, a California-based market research firm, that vaginal rings would see growth throughout the world.[11]

Depo-Provera shots are marketed to teens as a convenient method of birth control because they only have to see a doctor every three months to get the injection. With the shots, menstruation basically stops, and it can take women a long time to be fertile again after they stop. But that's not the worst of it. The feminist site Our Bodies Ourselves has quite a few posts about what happens to women once they stop getting Depo-Provera shots.

For example, women from across the globe who decided to stop the shots "experienced heavy and continuous bleeding, extreme breast tenderness, weight gain, headaches, nausea, extreme mood swings, depression, hair loss, and damaged relationships."[12]

---

[11]   "U.S. Contraceptive Market Size, Share & Trends Analysis Report By Product (Pills, Condoms, Vaginal Ring, Subdermal Implants, IUD, Injectable), And Segment Forecasts, 2020 – 2027," Grand View Research, December 2020, https://www.grandviewresearch.com/industry-analysis/us-contraceptive-market.

[12]   Laura Wershler, "'I Wouldn't Recommend It to Anyone': What We Can Learn from Women who have had Bad Experiences with

The reason? Hormonal chaos. The body was not made to be tinkered with in this way. Depo-Provera fools a woman's body into suppressing hormone production. When the shots are stopped, the body goes into overdrive to produce estrogen, but there's not enough progesterone being produced to counteract the estrogen.

According to OurBodiesOurselves.org, "Erratic, high, unopposed estrogen causes most of the miserable symptoms."[13]

If you're thinking you might as well just stick with the pill, please think again. There are too many different kinds of pills to list here, but all of them come with potentially serious side effects, like breast or cervical cancer, blood clots, heart attack, stroke, liver and gallbladder disease, and depression. They can also cause seizures and severe skin rashes.

The pills Yaz and Yasmin, both made by the pharmaceutical firm Bayer, have prompted more than ten thousand women to file lawsuits and led to more than one hundred deaths. As of 2016, according to DrugWatch.com, Bayer had paid out more than $2 billion to women who developed blood clots and pulmonary embolism; $21 million for gallbladder injuries, and nearly $57 million to settle claims of heart attacks and strokes.[14]

Depo-Provera," *Our Bodies, Our Blog*, August 24, 2016, https://www.ourbodiesourselves.org/2016/08/i-wouldnt-recommend-it-to-anyone-depo-provera/.

[13]   Ibid.

[14]   Michelle Llamas, "Yaz Lawsuits," Drugwatch, accessed November 30, 2021, https://www.drugwatch.com/yaz/lawsuits/.

Bayer paid an additional $20 million for a deceptive commercial that said Yaz and Yasmin were approved for and effective in combating premenstrual syndrome and acne. But those were lies, and the company got caught.

Further Concerns

If women's health and the damage these hormonal contraceptives do to their health is not enough to convince you not to go down this road, then here's just one more argument to consider: the effect on our environment.

The US Geological Survey did a study in 2015 that discovered freshwater fish in lakes, rivers, and streams are ingesting a hormone found in birth control pills. This affects their ability to produce offspring by as much as 30 percent.[15]

If all the medical and scientific studies aren't enough, let's look logically at the pill and what it does. Think about the human body for a moment. Of its many complex systems, the reproductive system—capable of conceiving and sustaining new human life—is the most "wondrously made" (cf. Ps 139). If you tinker with this system, for years or even decades, there very well could be consequences. Yes, hundreds of millions of women have taken the pill over the last sixty years and have not developed breast, cervical, or liver cancer, but hundreds of thousands have been harmed,

---

15   Ramji K. Bhandari, Frederick S. vom Saal, and Donald E. Tillitt, "Transgenerational effects from early developmental exposures to bisphenol A or 17α-ethinylestradiol in medaka, *Oryzias latipes*," *Scientific Reports*, March 20, 2015, https://www.nature.com/articl es/srep09303.

even killed, by swallowing the lie that avoiding pregnancy is worth any price.

The pill also wreaks havoc on women emotionally. Those of us who work for pro-life organizations have known for a long time that contraception and abortion go hand-in-hand. Dr. Theresa Burke, co-founder of the post-abortion healing ministry Rachel's Vineyard, discovered the link more than thirty years ago in her work:

> I never expected the subject of contraception linked to deep and hidden emotional pain to repeatedly sur-face during our weekends for healing after abortion. Many abortions are associated with a failure in con-traception. Any woman who leaves an abortion clinic is released with an arsenal of birth-control pills. The behavior that led to the pregnancy is never addressed, but she is armed with the resources to prevent another pregnancy . . . or so she thinks. Besides these obvious reasons for grief, I was rather astounded that a grow-ing number of women, including non-Catholics, were coming forward to say that they were also experiencing profound feelings of grief and loss because of contra-ceptive use which resulted in spontaneous abortions.[16]

I know what Dr. Burke says is true. Years after I stopped taking the pill, as I wrote about in the previous chapter, I found myself feeling guilty about the potential lives I ended by my contraceptive habits. I, too, had profound feelings of grief, which I later addressed on a Rachel's Vineyard retreat.

---

[16]   Theresa Burke, interview with author.

Dr. Peggy Hartshorn, chairman of the board of Heartbeat International, the first and one of the largest networks of pregnancy help organizations in the world, also noted the link between contraception and abortion years ago when she began helping women with unexpected pregnancies in the mid-1970s. She agrees with Dr. Burke that many abortions are associated with a failure in contraception:

> I was surprised at first to learn that almost every pregnant girl or woman I worked with had used some form of contraceptive, most often the Pill. Often they stopped because they hated the physical effects such as bloating, weight gain, and worse. Many women then and today express the thought that they did what they had been told is responsible and smart by using the Pill to prevent pregnancy. When they get pregnant anyway, they think it is responsible and smart to have an abortion. This is because they have become convinced that sexual intimacy can and should be separated from child-bearing entirely.[17]

Dr. Hartshorn says she became convinced that many women desperately need to learn the truth about their sexuality; this led to her development of the Sexual Integrity program, for use in the over two thousand pregnancy help centers in the USA. "The truth is that their femininity is based on their physical, emotional, intellectual, and spiritual wholeness as women, a giver and bearer of love and life. Being responsible

---

[17]   Peggy Hartshorn, interview with author.

does not mean taking the Pill or having an abortion. It means respecting oneself and one's God-given dignity as a woman."[18]

When you think of everything we know about hormonal contraception—increased risk of breast, cervical, ovarian, and other cancers; increased risks of blood clots, heart attacks, and strokes; increased risk of death; higher rates of divorce; emotional complications, and a negative impact on the environment—ask yourself if any of this is empowering to women.

Stay tuned, because in later chapters, we will talk about the empowering effects of chastity!

---

[18]   Ibid.

3

From Illegal to Legal Abortion: How Did We Get There?

Abortion through the Ages and Around the World

Attempts to terminate a pregnancy have been around since before the birth of Christ. In fact, the first recorded evidence of induced abortion is from Egypt in the year 1550 BC. Despite this long history, throughout the centuries, terminating a pregnancy—abortion—has had a negative connotation. Only in recent times have people viewed abortion as a sacred right, or even something to be celebrated.

In 1979, a women's health researcher published a study titled "Abortion in Early America," which summed up the abortion landscape from the seventeenth through the nineteenth centuries.

> Abortion was frequently practiced in North America during the period from 1600 to 1900. Many tribal societies knew how to induce abortions. They used a variety of methods including the use of black root and cedar root as abortifacient agents. During the colonial

3

period, the legality of abortion varied from colony to colony and reflected the attitude of the European country which controlled the specific colony. In the British colonies abortions were legal if they were performed prior to quickening.[1] In the French colonies abortions were frequently performed despite the fact that they were considered to be illegal. In the Spanish and Portuguese colonies abortion was illegal. From 1776 until the mid-1800s abortion was viewed as socially unacceptable; however, abortions were not illegal in most states. During the 1860s a number of states passed anti-abortion laws. Most of these laws were ambiguous and difficult to enforce. After 1860 stronger anti-abortion laws were passed and these laws were more vigorously enforced. As a result, many women began to utilize illegal underground abortion services.[2]

Legal abortion outside the United States began in 1920, with a very interesting historical footnote. As most Catholics are aware, the Blessed Mother appeared to three children in Fatima, Portugal in 1917, the same year that a revolution began in Russia that would lead that nation, and much of that part of the world, into communism. One of Mary's messages was, "Russia will spread its errors throughout the world." Three years later, Russia became the first country to legalize abortion.

---

[1]   "Quickening" is when the mother feels the baby for the first time.
[2]   Z. Acevedo, "Abortion in Early America," *Women Health* 4, no.2 (Summer 1979), pp. 159–67.

It would be another thirty years before a second country—North Korea—followed suit. From 1950 to 1965, only communist nations made it legal to kill children in the womb. These included Hungary, many of the nations that were then part of the Soviet Union, and Cuba, a Roman Catholic country under the dictatorship of communist leader Fidel Castro.

Denmark and Tunisia joined the United States in legalizing abortion in 1973. Most of the world's recognized 195 nations now have some form of legal abortion, with most of them offering it to women by request. However, abortion through all nine months is available only in a handful of countries, including the United States, Canada, China, North Korea, Vietnam, Singapore, and the Netherlands.[3] In much of Europe, abortion is only legal until twelve weeks.[4]

Abortion in the United Sates

Abortion laws began to be relaxed across the United States years before *Roe v. Wade* made it legal. In 1967, three states—Colorado, followed by North Carolina and California—made abortion legal if a woman got pregnant from

---

[3]   Michelle Ye Hee Lee, "Is the United States one of seven countries that 'allow elective abortions after 20 weeks of pregnancy?'" *The Washington Post*, October 9, 2017, https://www.washingtonpost .com/news/fact-checker/wp/2017/10/09/is-the-united-states-one -of-seven-countries-that-allow-elective-abortions-after-20-weeks -of-pregnancy/.

[4]   "European Abortion Laws: A Comparative Overview," Center for Reproductive Rights, accessed November 15, 2021, https://repro ductiverights.org/wp-content/uploads/2020/12/European-abor tion-law-a-comparative-review.pdf.

rape or incest, or if continuing the pregnancy would seriously impair her health. Oregon followed suit in 1969.

In 1970, Hawaii became the first state to allow abortion at the request of the mother. That same year, New York legalized abortion until twenty-four weeks.

By 1972, thirteen states had laws like Colorado's, and when *Roe* was decided in 1973, abortion was illegal in thirty states and legal in various circumstances in the remaining twenty.

In order to understand how *Roe v. Wade* and the companion case, *Doe v. Bolton*, were decided on January 22, 1973, legalizing abortion through all nine months of pregnancy, we have to go back and take a look at the major players leading up to that event.

Dr. Bernard Nathanson was licensed to practice medicine in New York state in 1952 and became board certified in obstetrics and gynecology in 1960. He was named director of the Center for Reproductive and Sexual Health (CRASH), which at that time billed itself as the largest freestanding abortion facility in the world.

Nathanson was one of the founding members of the National Association for the Repeal of Abortion Laws, a radically pro-abortion organization now known as NARAL Pro-Choice America. NARAL joined hands with the National Organization for Women and its leader, Betty Friedan, to push for legal abortion. Working with them was a man named Larry Lader, who became convinced that abortion was the solution to overpopulation while he was writing a biography of eugenicist and Planned Parenthood founder Margaret Sanger.

But just a year after his efforts to legalize abortion had come to fruition, Dr. Nathanson wrote in the *New England Journal of Medicine*, "I am deeply troubled by my own increasing certainty that I had in fact presided over 60,000 deaths." He went on to claim that he had personally performed five thousand abortions, one of whom was his own child.[5]

I had the privilege, along with Father Frank Pavone of Priests for Life, of meeting and getting to know Dr. Nathanson. He told us how he and others convinced the media, lawmakers, and members of the public to support efforts to legalize abortion in America. They did this by lying. They came up with the number ten thousand to describe the number of women dying annually from illegal or do-it-yourself abortions. The media reported that number without ever trying to confirm it. In reality, the number was much lower.

According to the National Center for Vital Statistics, the number of maternal deaths due to abortion in 1968 was ninety-nine. Across the next four years, that number fluctuated from as low as twenty-five to just over one hundred.[6] A far cry from ten thousand, but the lie helped Dr. Nathanson and his colleagues to accomplish their mission of legalizing abortion in all fifty states.

Dr. Nathanson also blamed the clergy for making his job easier. He said the Church in America was asleep and that

---

[5]   This is a story that quotes his 1974 essay in the *New England Journal of Medicine*. The journal article itself is only available to subscribers. Robert P. George, "Bernard Nathanson: A Life Transformed by Truth," Public Discourse, February 27, 2011, https://www.thepublicdiscourse.com/2011/02/2806/.

[6]   National Vital Statistics System, Centers for Disease Control and Prevention, https://www.cdc.gov/nchs/nvss/index.htm.

if the clergy had been "united, purposeful and strong," the movement to legalize abortion would never have succeeded.

It was the development of ultrasound, which allowed Dr. Nathanson to observe an abortion in real time, that led him to reconsider his views. He performed his last abortion sometime in late 1978 or 1979. From there, he became an outspoken pro-life activist who converted to Catholicism in 1996 during a private baptism with Cardinal John O'Connor, leader of the Archdiocese of New York.

He is often quoted as saying abortion is "the most atrocious holocaust *in the history of the United States.*" In his book *Aborting America,* he first exposed what he called "the dishonest beginnings of the abortion movement."[7] In 1984, he directed and narrated a film titled *The Silent Scream,* in cooperation with the National Right to Life Committee, which contained the ultrasound video of an abortion at twelve weeks. To watch it on YouTube, you have to sign in to Google to ensure you are old enough to see it. It is considered too disturbing for young people, and yet I know girls who were as young as thirteen when they had their abortions.

Referring to his previous work as an abortion provider and abortion rights activist, he wrote in his 1996 autobiography, *Hand of God,* "I am one of those who helped usher in this barbaric age."[8]

---

[7]   Bernard Nathanson, *Aborting America* (Pinnacle Books, 1981).

[8]   Bernard Nathanson, *The Hand of God: A Journey from Death to Life from the Abortion Doctor Who Changed His Mind* (Salem Books, 2013).

All those who orchestrated the effort to bring abortion on demand to America believed it would be empowering for women, but you will see that it is just the opposite.

Meet Roe and Doe

Who are the women for whom the two abortion cases, *Roe v. Wade* and *Doe v. Bolton*, were named?

First, let's meet Norma McCorvey (a.k.a. Jane Roe).

In 1969, Norma McCorvey was a Texas woman in her early twenties, and she was pregnant for a third time. She was working with an adoption lawyer when two young abortion-rights lawyers—Sarah Weddington and Linda Coffey—came into her life. Norma was essentially homeless when the two attorneys learned of her situation. They treated her to a pizza lunch, and Norma signed the documents that allowed them to exploit her as a way to legalize abortion. She became "Jane Roe" because she didn't want her name in the papers. Little did she know how famous, or infamous, Jane Roe would one day become, or how often her own name would appear in the press still to this day.

By the time she met Weddington and Coffey, Norma already had two children and a failed marriage, with a family history of abuse and addiction. Norma was unable to abort her third child because Texas only allowed abortion to save a mother's life.

Although Norma would never have an abortion, her lawyer Sarah Weddington did, and that experience played a central role in opening the door to a decision that led to the death of now more than sixty-two million children.

In 1967, Sarah and her then-boyfriend Ron Weddington, both law students at the time, were facing an unplanned pregnancy that threatened to disrupt their plans. To solve the problem, the couple drove south to an abortion clinic in Piedra Negras, Mexico. In her memoir *A Question of Choice*, Sarah wrote that upon waking after the procedure, she thought, "I hope I don't die, and I pray that no one ever finds out about this."[9]

For twenty-five years, their abortion remained a dark secret. Only in the writing of her memoir did she finally open up about her own abortion. Her autobiography presents Weddington as a serious woman with workaholic tendencies. One of her motivations in seeking to legalize abortion throughout the United States was very likely a desire to validate her own choice in ending the life of her child.

In 1970, Coffee and Weddington filed a lawsuit on behalf of Jane Roe against Henry Wade, then the district attorney of Dallas County in the US District Court for the Northern District of Texas. In June 1970, the court ruled that the state's abortion ban was illegal because it violated a constitutional right to privacy. The case eventually was appealed to the US Supreme Court. Meanwhile, McCorvey gave birth and made an adoption plan for her child.

Just before the Texas case went to trial, Sandra Cano, a woman in Georgia whose life was even more chaotic than Norma's, was taken under the wing of another lawyer looking to legalize abortion.

---

[9]   Sarah Weddington, *A Question of Choice* (The Feminist Press at CUNY, 2013).

In April 1970, pregnant with her fourth child, with two of her children in foster care and a third placed with an adoptive family, her husband in and out of jail for child molestation, Sandra went to the Atlanta Legal Aid Office for help with getting a divorce and regaining custody of her two children in foster care. She wasn't even looking for an abortion.

Sandra was introduced to attorney Margie Pitts Hames, and the same kind of manipulation going on in Texas with Norma McCorvey started up in Georgia with the woman who would come to be known as Mary Doe.

On behalf of her client, Hames joined a lawsuit filed in the District Court for the Northern District of Georgia to have the abortion law in Georgia overturned. At the time, abortion was only legal for rape or if the mother's life was in danger, or in the case of a severe fetal anomaly. The court found that among several people listed as plaintiffs, only Sandra had the legal right to bring the case because her privacy rights had been violated by not allowing her to have the abortion (even though she had never wanted one!). In the case named *Doe v. Bolton*, the court struck down parts of the Georgia abortion law and upheld others.

A court document in that case indicated that Sandra had tried to have an abortion at a hospital in Atlanta but was turned down. Like so much of this case, the story of being turned away for an abortion was a lie made up by Sandra's legal team, who recognized in Sandra the same things Norma's lawyers had in Texas: these were women who could be manipulated.

The documents for the Georgia case included an affidavit signed by Sandra. But eighteen years later, when both she and Norma were trying to get the decisions in their cases reversed, Sandra saw the affidavit and realized she had signed it without knowing what it said. She had trusted her legal team. That was Sandra's biggest mistake.

Prior to her case going before the judge, Sandra was scheduled for an abortion she never wanted; her lawyers even raised the money. Instead of ending the life of her child, she ran away, boarding a bus for Hugo, Oklahoma, where her in-laws lived. She agreed to return for the hearing only after securing promises that she would not be forced to abort her baby. She gave birth to that child on November 7, 1970, and made an adoption plan.

Lawyers for both cases, *Roe v. Wade* in Texas and *Doe v. Bolton* in Georgia, were unsatisfied with the outcome of their efforts to legalize abortion throughout the United States, so both cases climbed their way up to the US Supreme Court.

Roe v. Wade and *Doe v. Bolton* were argued on December 13, 1971, but because the court was short two justices due to retirements, the cases were argued again on October 11, 1972.

On January 22, 1973, seven justices (all "old, white men" according to the woke descriptions of today) found that women in the United States have a fundamental right to choose abortion without government interference. Two justices dissented, Byron White and Chief Justice William Rehnquist. The court struck down the Texas law banning abortion, invalidated what remained of the Georgia law, and legalized the procedure nationwide.

To this day, January 22 is a day of infamy in the United States, mourned and protested by pro-lifers and celebrated by pro-abortion advocates and those who profit from the death of babies in the womb.

Margie Pitts Hames phoned Sandra with the news, while Norma read it in the Dallas newspaper.

Testifying before the Senate Judiciary Committee's Subcommittee on the Constitution in 2005, Sandra said, "Doe has been a nightmare. Over the last 32 years, I have become a prisoner of the case."[10] Two years earlier, she tried to reopen the case, saying she had not been aware at the time that the case had been filed on her behalf. Federal district and circuit courts denied her application for review, as did the US Supreme Court.

Allan Parker, president and founder of the Justice Foundation in San Antonio, Texas, represented Norma and Sandra as they tried to overturn the *Roe* and *Doe* cases. This is, as far as I know, the first time in American history that two people who *won* their landmark cases tried to have them overturned. Unfortunately, the Supreme Court would not hear their case.

Both Norma and Sandra died recently; Norma on February 18, 2017, at the age of sixty-nine, and Sandra on September 14, 2014, at the age of sixty-six.

---

[10]   *Testimony of Sandra Cano before the Subcommittee on the Constitution of the Senate Judiciary Committee*, June 23, 2005, https://www.judiciary.senate.gov/imo/media/doc/Cano%20Testimony%2062305.pdf.

Revealing the Personal Dimension

In looking at the history of any movement, along with the information one can gain from research or written records, there is also the personal dimension: Who knew the people involved? What insights into their personalities can be learned from their friends? What happened behind the scenes that the historical records didn't capture?

In this regard, I am privileged to be able to say that I knew some of the key people we have been speaking about, so join me for a few moments for a front-row seat behind the scenes.

As I mentioned previously, I knew Dr. Bernard Nathanson, who, before his death in 2011, strongly supported the work of Priests for Life. He was convinced, as we already saw, that activating the clergy was and still is one of the keys to stopping the culture of death. He was brutally honest in sharing what he had done to, as he described it, "uncage the abortion monster in the United States."[11] He often talked to us about the bioethical challenges we would face in the twenty-first century, predicting like a prophet in the late 1990s the exact headlines we read today regarding stem cells, genetic research, and more. He told us he wanted to become a bioethicist so that he could stay ahead of the curve of what the culture of death was doing. Father Frank and I were with him when he announced publicly his intention to convert to the Catholic faith, and we saw his sincerity and desire for God's forgiveness.

---

[11] Bernard Nathanson, personal conversation with author. Dr. Nathanson also said this in many of his talks throughout the years.

Just days before Dr. Nathanson died, Father Frank visited him in his New York City apartment. He was confined to his bed and could not talk beyond a whisper. The first thing he said to Father Frank was, "How goes the crusade?" In other words, his mind was not on himself or his sufferings; it was on the great pro-life cause, of which he knew Father Frank and I were leaders, and which he wanted to succeed in order to undo some of the damage he himself had unleashed.

Norma McCorvey and Sandra Cano were very similar in many ways—simple, practical, down-to-earth women, opposed to abortion but vulnerable to manipulation. Both were used by the abortion industry.

We gave them many opportunities to be together with one another. Both of them became dear friends. I spent much more time with Norma, staying at her home in Dallas and hosting her at mine (she called me the "Woman of the East"). During one of my visits to her home, she took me shopping for my first pair of cowboy boots and a cowboy hat, which I still have today and cherish as a keepsake from our friendship. She loved New York bagels, and when she had a craving for them, she would call me and ask me to send her some. Onion bagels were among her favorites.

Both Norma and Sandra detested abortion and grieved every single day the damage being done by the Supreme Court decisions in which they were plaintiffs. They lived a daily battle to minimize the damage and to reverse those decisions. We provided them legal help, platforms to share their stories, ways to be part of the pro-life movement nationally and around the world, and opportunities to heal.

Among the many public events we shared together, Norma and Sandra both came to be with me and Father Frank when he was honored by the National Right to Life Committee in 2001 with their highest award, as well as the following year when the Franciscan University of Steubenville gave Father Frank an honorary doctorate. We also brought both of them to the National Memorial for the Unborn in Chattanooga, Tennessee, where they publicly mourned the babies who had been killed by their court decisions and set up a plaque calling for the reversal of those decisions.

These and many other moments with them were witnessed by others in the pro-life cause. But even more significant and frequent were the "behind the scenes" moments we lived through with them, when the cameras were off, the crowds dispersed, and the events had ended. These are the moments that reveal how real their daily pain was as they lived with the reality of abortion and their involvement with it. These are the moments when we saw their deepest despair as well as their deepest faith. Norma, for instance, would take consolation in how the statue of Mary in her backyard made her heart leap to Jesus. And when we would visit her home, we saw that she had a hobby of making rosaries at her dining room table. These acts of faith gave her the joy of knowing she could bring someone else to the loving mercy of Christ.

Unforgettable, too, were the moments on the Rachel's Vineyard retreat that Norma made when she came face-to-face on a deeper level with her pain over abortion. She would literally run out of the chapel, struggling to face God, before quietly returning later with even greater fervor to seek His face and His peace. This was a daily struggle, and we walked with her through it for years on end.

In fact, Father Frank and I were on a business trip to Rome when we received a call from Norma's daughter Melissa. We had known that Norma was very ill, but now learned that death was imminent. We spoke to Norma within an hour of her passing away, when she told us to continue the fight to bring an end to abortion.

I can honestly say that there was never a conversation I had with Norma where we did not laugh. God allowed us all to rejoice in His kindness, to look always at the positive side of our journeys and our struggles, and to find humor as His gift.

Father Frank and I remain ever grateful that as we intersected with these remarkable people of history, in the very years that it was being made, we were able to also interact as friends.

The Power of the Law

I hope you understand that legalized abortion in America was built on many, many lies. We saw that abortion has been around since 1550 BC, but until it became legal, it was frowned upon. Laws change behavior and keep things in check. For example, we have different speeding laws in our country, and yes, there are people who do not pay attention to speed limits and drive very fast. But knowing it is illegal to drive over a certain speed keeps most drivers from speeding. It's also against the law to steal. Do people still steal? Of course. But the number of people who steal is far lower than it would be if stealing was legal. You get the point.

Many women would never have considered abortion if it wasn't legal to obtain one. I know this firsthand because I cofounded the Silent No More Awareness Campaign, where women who have gone through healing from their abortion tell the story about how abortion damaged them. We will look at the physical and psychological problems with abortion in later chapters, but the point I want to make right now is that many of these women have said that if abortion had not been legal, they probably would not have had one.

Leslie Blackwell was a woman I met through Silent No More. She had two abortions, the first when she was just out of college and had landed her dream job in broadcast journalism. "Regarding the legality of abortion, the fact it was legal in the late '70s was a safety net tucked in the recesses of my mind," she said. "I knew I'd have an out if I got pregnant, not that I wanted to. Because abortion was legal, I believe I engaged in more promiscuous behavior because I knew my 'problem' could be eradicated if needed."[12]

Jody Duffy was twenty-one years old and was a newly commissioned second lieutenant in the Army when she discovered she was pregnant after a date rape in 1980. She had recently been stationed in Arizona and wasn't sure where to turn or what to do. There were very few single moms among female soldiers, although by then the military did not discharge pregnant women.

---

[12]   Leslie Blackwell, personal conversation with the author. Leslie came to regret both of those abortions. You can read more stories of these women at www.abortiontestimony.com.

Another solider stationed with her in Arizona found a doctor in Tucson, and the two of them made the eighty-mile drive to abort Jody's baby.

"After he told me he had made the appointment, I said, 'OK, I guess that's what I'm going to do.' It came too easy," Jody told me. "It was all too easy. If abortion had not been legal, I wouldn't have known what to do or where to go. I think I would have tried to keep the baby or made an adoption plan."[13]

So you can see how laws shape people's lives. The sad history of the legalization of abortion in the United States has led to the slaughter of millions of children. Good and hardworking people are now trying to use the law to reverse these horrible rulings, and have made some progress since the days of the *Roe* and *Doe* cases.

But the law is not the only way we can put an end to this genocide. Science is also a friend of the pro-life cause. Notice that many of the women I mentioned in this chapter didn't know they were carrying a human life in their womb. By educating young people about the reality of the life that comes from a pregnancy (even if the pregnancy is unwanted), we can show people the true tragedy of abortion. So let us turn next to science and meet the unborn child.

---

[13]   Jody Duffy, personal conversation with author.

4

Meet the Unborn Child

Who Is the Unborn?

The outcome of every abortion is the violent death of the most innocent victim: an unborn child. The word *unborn* has two meanings. In one sense, it refers to all those who will be born, no matter how far into the future. Those to be born a hundred years from now are, in that sense, "unborn." But the word also refers to those who have not yet been born but already exist and are living and growing as unique human beings in their mother's womb. Those are the children we are discussing in this chapter.

Seeing the Unborn

In 1973, when *Roe v. Wade* and *Doe v. Bolton* were decided, ultrasound was not being used routinely in medical practices. In fact, in the *Roe* decision, US Supreme Court justice Harry Blackmun wrote, "We need not resolve the difficult question of when life begins. When those trained in the respective disciplines of medicine, philosophy, and theology are unable to arrive at any consensus, the judiciary, at this point in the development of man's knowledge, is not in a position to speculate as to the answer."

The seven justices who voted in favor of legalizing abortion throughout pregnancy decided not to delve too deeply into science. If you would like to know why, I recommend you read *The Fake and Deceptive Science Behind Roe v. Wade* by Dr. Thomas Hilgers.[1]

Early sonogram pictures of children in the womb were fuzzy at best, and weren't routinely in use until the late 1970s. Mothers didn't even know the sex of their unborn child until the day of delivery. I didn't even know I was having twins until late in my second pregnancy!

This is quite different from today, when most parents want to know as soon as possible the sex of their baby, and they see him or her on several ultrasounds before delivery. Moms, dads, and grandparents start showing those ultrasound pictures around to their friends. You see the pictures on their refrigerators, framed on desks in their offices, and of course these pictures are the first ones added to the baby's scrapbook.

Ultrasound makes it hard for abortion supporters to argue that the unborn child is somehow not fully alive. But the evidence for this living, growing human being can be seen long before the first ultrasound appointment.

---

[1]   Thomas Hilgers, *The Fake and Deceptive Science Behind Roe v. Wade* (Beaufort Books, 2020).

Journey of the Unborn

A groundbreaking video called "The Biology of Prenatal Development," produced by the Endowment for Human Development and distributed by National Geographic, describes in incredible detail—with images from inside the womb—what takes place from the moment of fertilization until birth. According to this video, which is grounded only in science, "the dynamic process by which the single-cell zygote becomes a 100 trillion cell adult is perhaps the most remarkable phenomenon in all of nature."

Following fertilization, or the joining of the egg (oocyte) and sperm (spermatozoan), a new single-cell organism called a zygote is formed. The word means "yoked" or "joined." The zygote is "the unique first edition of a new individual's complete genetic blueprint."[2] All your DNA is now present, and that's what makes you who you are, a unique individual.

Within twenty-four to thirty hours, the zygote has completed its first cell division. This cell division continues as the zygote completes its journey through the mother's fallopian tubes. At six days after fertilization, the zygote begins to embed itself in the inner wall of the mother's uterus. By ten to twelve days, implantation is complete and the cells on the outside edge of the zygote begin to create the placenta, which will nourish this new individual throughout the pregnancy. According to the Endowment for Human Development, an organization that offers prenatal education, "The

---

[2]   "Multilingual Illustrated DVD: The Biology of Prenatal Development," The Endowment for Human Development, accessed November 15, 2021, https://www.ehd.org/resources_bpd_illustrated.php?page=1.

life support systems of the placenta rival those of intensive care units of modern hospitals."[3]

By three weeks after fertilization, the brain begins dividing into three sections, and the respiratory and digestive systems begin to form. By three to four weeks, the heart emerges and grows rapidly. Three weeks and one day after fertilization, the heart begins to beat.

Week four is characterized by rapid brain growth. The heart beats 113 times per minute. Five weeks in, the cerebral hemisphere of the brain appears. This is where thoughts, memories, speech, vision, hearing, voluntary movement, and problem-solving begin. Early reproductive cells and hand plates develop.

By six weeks after fertilization, spontaneous and reflexive movements are noted. The ears start to take shape and primitive brain waves are detected. By six-and-a-half weeks, distinct elbows and hand movements can be seen. By seven-and-a-half weeks, the ovaries are detectable in females, the eyelids are growing, and the fingers are separated.

Look how much of the unique unborn child has developed as the child's mom is just discovering she is pregnant! If this pregnancy is unwanted, this is often when the abortion decision is made, but mothers who watch this video will clearly see this is not a clump of cells they are thinking of aborting.

Let's continue looking at this remarkable unborn child. By the seven-and-a-half-week mark, the brain is highly

---

[3]   Ibid., "0 – 4 Weeks," https://www.ehd.org/resources_bpd_illustra ted.php?page=6.

complex, the embryo can roll over, bring his hand to his face, rotate his head, move his jaw, point his toes, and make grasping motions. Seventy-five percent of babies will exhibit right-hand dominance by this time. This baby's heart has already beat over 7 million times since its first flutter at three weeks and one day after fertilization.

By eight weeks and two days, the bones, joints, and muscles closely resemble those of adults. This marks the end of the embryonic period and the beginning of the fetal period, which will continue until birth. The single-cell organism created after fertilization now has nearly one billion cells and four thousand distinct anatomic structures—90 percent of the structures found in adults. Lightly touching the fetus at this stage causes the baby to squint.

At nine weeks, the baby begins to suck his thumb, can grasp an object, sigh, stretch, and respond to light touch. In females, the uterus has become identifiable.

A burst of growth marks the transition from nine to ten weeks, with the fetus increasing his body weight by 75 percent during this time. The baby can yawn, roll her eyes, and open and close her mouth. Fingernails and toenails begin to develop, and the unique fingerprints that will identify this particular human being throughout his or her life are already present.

The nose and lips are fully formed by the eleventh week, and by twelve weeks, which marks the end of the first trimester, the entire body of the fetus, except the back and top of the head, responds to light touch. Also, bowel movements have begun.

At fourteen weeks, females move their jaws much more than males. Also, stimulation near the mouth prompts the fetus to turn toward the touch with an open mouth. This is the earliest sign of the rooting reflex that helps a baby find his mother's nipple.

It is at fourteen weeks that many doctors do more extensive tests and special ultrasounds in the hospital, and it is at this point that many parents can find out the sex of their baby if they choose to know ahead of time.[4]

Couples who want to know the sex of their baby sometimes host "gender reveal" parties, inviting friends and family to a special celebration to declare if it's a boy or a girl. These parties are getting increasingly elaborate. One family in New Jersey staged a wrestling match between men dressed in either pink or blue tutus and tights. Pink won. Many couples announce the name they have chosen for their new son or daughter during this gender reveal party.

But fourteen weeks also can be life-threatening or even life-ending for babies in the womb. Fetal abnormalities like Down syndrome, spina bifida, cystic fibrosis, and other problems can be diagnosed (or often misdiagnosed) by this point. This is when many doctors will "counsel" the couple about termination (a.k.a., abortion)! It's tragic that this baby now becomes a child whose life is in jeopardy. We will talk about this more later, but let's get back to the discovery of this amazing, unique human being.

---

[4]   From babycenter.com: If you have a prenatal blood test (NIPT), you may be able to find out your baby's sex as early as eleven weeks of pregnancy. Ultrasounds may reveal sex organs by fourteen weeks, but they aren't considered fully accurate until eighteen weeks. If you have CVS at ten weeks, the results will reveal your baby's sex by twelve weeks.

Between fourteen and eighteen weeks, mothers begin to feel stirring in their womb as their rapidly growing babies move around. Many moms describe this as a fluttering feeling.

By nineteen weeks, the heartbeat begins to pattern itself to circadian rhythms that follow a roughly twenty-four-hour cycle in response to light and darkness, and the fetus will respond to a growing range of sounds by five months. Many moms begin to sing to their baby, and of course, the baby hears his parent's voices. I started speaking to my grandchildren when they were in utero too!

At twenty-two weeks, considered the beginning of the age of viability, the lungs have the capacity to breathe air. Fetuses can blink at six months, and the startle reflex is observed, particularly in females. By six months and three weeks, the brain is growing rapidly.

The eyes can produce tears at twenty-six weeks, and pupils respond to light the very next week.

By now, all components for the sense of smell are operational. Also, introducing a sweet substance into the amniotic fluid leads to more swallowing, while a bitter substance causes the fetus to swallow less. Changing facial expressions and somersaults are some of the new skills developing at this time.

High- and low-pitched sounds prompt a response at twenty-eight weeks. And two weeks later, the central nervous system becomes increasingly complex. By thirty-two weeks, true alveoli, or air pockets, form in the lungs. They will continue to grow until a child is eight years old.

By thirty-five weeks, the fetus has a firm hand grasp. At thirty-eight weeks past fertilization, the fetus sends out the hormone estrogen to begin labor. And soon our baby will begin the journey down the birth canal to make his or her grand entrance.

That's how every one of us began. Whether babies are welcomed or unwanted, the scientific facts about that child remain the same.[5]

The Education Resource Fund's embryo and fetus pictures featured in this book (see photo section) are derived from many smaller images that have been "stitched" together. If you want to see more pictures of the developing child, go to Unborn.info.

But after reading this and checking out all these images, you might be asking, how does abortion fit into this baby picture? In the next chapter, we will look at exactly what abortion does to an unborn child.

---

[5]   The wording used in this book for the medical details of the baby's development was taken from the "My Baby App," which can be downloaded in the app store for iPhones and Androids.

5

What Is an Abortion?

Misleading Words and Euphemisms

In this chapter, we will discuss exactly what abortion is and the violent procedures used to end the lives of children in the womb. Here's the way abortion is defined in the Google dictionary: "The deliberate termination of a human pregnancy, most often performed during the first 28 weeks of pregnancy."[1]

That definition, while technically correct, doesn't even begin to tell the truth about abortion. The child whose death is the aim of every abortion isn't even mentioned. Here's what abortion really is: *the deliberate execution of a separate, whole, and unique human being.*

You were once a whole, separate, and unique human being in your mother's womb. If you were born after January 22, 1973, you are here not because the laws in our country protected you but because your parents chose to let you be born. You were a wanted and probably welcomed child. If you haven't already seen your ultrasound pictures, ask your

---

[1]   Google dictionary, s.v., "abortion," accessed November 15, 2021.

parents to show you. The pictures of you inside your mother's womb were your first baby pictures!

The pro-abortion lobby likes to say abortion is a "vital part of reproductive healthcare," overlooking the obvious fact that a pregnant woman is the definition of reproductive health. While it's certainly true that some women do not want to have children, it doesn't change the fact that women's bodies were built to conceive and grow and nourish new life. That's basic biology.

Abortion advocates also like to say that abortion is "reproductive justice," a term I have never understood. Does it mean women have to be able to kill our children to level the playing field with men? Is it fair to demand that form of justice from the innocent unborn? Abortion has allowed men to literally walk away if their girlfriend becomes pregnant with their child. She is already a mom and he is already a dad. Like it or not, that is a fact! So a dad who walks away is allowing the death of his unborn child!

The abortion industry often uses the power of language and euphemisms, twisting words to their advantage. They don't want to say what abortion actually is, so they get creative and soften the reality with terms like "reproductive justice" and "reproductive rights" and "pro-choice." But these terms don't convey what abortion actually is. Let's now talk about what abortion is and how it is performed.

The Morning-After Pill

More than sixty-two million children have died from abortion since *Roe v. Wade* made the procedure legal in 1973 (let that statistic sink in for a minute). These millions of children were killed in the womb in a variety of ways. One of these ways can take place as soon as a man's sperm fertilizes a woman's egg.

You may have heard of the morning-after pill or emergency contraception. It is called the "morning-after" pill because you take it after you have had unprotected sex. There are two drugs available to women and girls if they have had unprotected sex and don't want to have a baby.

Levonogestrel is sold under two brand names, Plan B and Next Choice One Dose. Both are available in pharmacies without a prescription to those fifteen and older and can be taken up to seventy-two hours after unprotected sex. Both of them work one of three ways: they can prevent ovulation, which is when an egg is released by a woman's fallopian tube; they can block the sperm from fertilizing the egg; or they can prevent the fertilized egg from implanting in the uterine wall.

Abortion sellers like Planned Parenthood and even government health organizations assert that Levonogestrel does not cause abortion, and they get away with that claim because of the definition of when pregnancy begins (again, getting creative with words). You remember from chapter 2 that the birth control pill was approved by the federal Food and Drug Administration in 1960, but in those early years, it was only available to married couples. In 1965, anticipating the day the pill would be available to all women—and because the pill also can prevent implantation of a fertilized egg—the American College of Obstetricians and Gynecologists changed the starting date for pregnancy. From then on, conception was considered to have taken place once the fertilized egg had implanted in the uterine wall.

But Catholics and pro-lifers do not accept that implantation—which can take place up to five days after fertilization—is when life begins. Once the sperm has fertilized the egg, a zygote is formed, and it contains all the genetic information for that brand new human being. *That* is when life begins. If Plan B prevents the fertilized egg, or zygote, from implanting, it is causing an abortion; yes, a very early abortion, but an abortion nonetheless.

Another drug, ulapristal acetate, which is sold under the brand name Ella, can be taken up to five days, or 120 hours, following unprotected sex. It works the same way as Plan B, but the chances are much greater in those later days that a woman or girl will be aborting a fertilized egg.

Side effects of both Plan B and Ella include dizziness, abdominal pain, nausea, and fatigue.[2] Both drugs can interact with prescription medication and street drugs a woman might be taking, meaning pregnancy can occur. Both Plan B and Ella are less effective for women who are overweight or obese. Also, since neither drug is 100 percent successful even if all the right conditions are met, a woman might still be pregnant after taking it.

While it may be true that, in some cases, taking the morning-after pill is different from going to get an actual abortion, since it is possible that no fertilization has taken place (and therefore there is no baby to abort), it is still wrong. For

---

[2]   "Ella – Uses, Side Effects, and More," WebMD, accessed November 15, 2021, https://www.webmd.com/drugs/2/drug-154978/ella-oral/details.

one, it could be that fertilization *did* take place and a child *was* killed. Secondly, we must consider the intention of an act when we determine the morality of it. Even if taking the morning-after pill did not result in a child being killed, *the intention was to kill a child*. The "just in case" nature of the act makes it no less problematic.

The Abortion Pill: Chemical and "Medication" Abortions

Now let's move past the morning-after pill. You have probably heard of a different pill—the "abortion pill." This can be a confusing term. It does not refer to Ella or Plan B but instead to what used to be known as RU-486. Now more commonly known as "chemical abortion" or "medication abortion," it is growing in popularity in the United States and throughout the world. Up to 40 percent of babies killed by abortion in the United States are now the victims of chemical abortion. Pro-lifers reject the term *medication abortion* because *a drug that kills a human being is not medicine*.

Chemical abortion was approved for use in the United States in 2000. It involves two drugs, mifepristone and misoprostol. The first drug—mifepristone—is designed to kill the baby in the womb; misoprostol then begins contractions that will lead to the dead baby being expelled from his or her mother. The drugs can be taken up to the tenth week of pregnancy.

Pro-abortion people like to say this type of abortion is easy and it's no big deal. But that's not the reality. It is an hours-long or even days-long procedure that leaves a mother bleeding and in pain. Often, she sees the tiny body of her baby as it passes out of her body. Her own home, in a sense, has become an abortion mill. She has now become the abortion doctor because she is the one taking the pills that kill her unborn child.

Many of the women who are part of the Silent No More Awareness Campaign have gone through the excruciating procedure. Here are just a few of their stories.[3]

Patricia in North Carolina was already the mother of a seven-month-old when she became involved in a new relationship with a "carefree twenty-two-year-old." She was six weeks pregnant when she went to Planned Parenthood and decided to have a chemical abortion.

The Planned Parenthood doctor told her there was nothing to worry about, that she would have "some bleeding and possibly clotting," but that more severe side effects were rare.

Patricia tells a different story (please be aware that what follows is very difficult to read):

> The next day, at home alone with my infant son, I took the abortion pills. Within one hour I knew that everything the doctor had told me was a lie. I was bleeding so heavily, I believed I was dying. I was passing clots the size of baseballs, and I was in the worst physical pain of my life, worse than childbirth. The worst part of my experience was when I was sitting on the toilet

---

[3]   These stories and more can be found on the Silent No More website. Please be aware that many of these stories are difficult to read and require some graphic detail.

and I felt myself pass a clot that felt strange. I looked into the toilet and saw my baby. It had a head, body, and tiny arms and legs. The shame and guilt that I felt at that moment, as I was forced to flush my aborted baby down the toilet, is impossible to describe.

Jessica in Oregon wrote this testimony about her chemical abortion that began at Planned Parenthood:

> They gave me one pill to take there and another to take at home hours later. I cried hysterically for the hour drive home, wondering how I could be so cruel to kill my own baby. I was so disgusted with myself after I took the pill. Not long after I took the second pill I felt nauseous and lightheaded, and stomach cramps started. I felt so weak that I just wanted to lay down, but I was in excruciating pain with heavy bleeding, and I felt that sitting on the toilet was best. I birthed my dead baby into my toilet. I was heartbroken when I saw that it had tiny fingers and toes. I bled a lot, and the abortion was excruciatingly painful, almost as painful as my two unmedicated full-term births.[4]

Chemical abortion is not a quick and simple procedure. Nor is it a safe one. The FDA has reported that twenty-four women died after chemical abortion and four thousand have been injured as of 2018.[5] But in a demonstration of

---

[4] You can read many more of these stories at www.abortiontestimony.com.

[5] "Mifepristone U.S. Post-Marketing Adverse Events Summary through 12/31/2018," Food and Drug Administration, accessed November 15, 2021, https://www.fda.gov/media/112118/download#:~:text=These%20 fatal%20cases%20were%20associated,%E2%80%9Cmultivisceral%20

how powerful the abortion lobby is in the United States, the FDA is no longer keeping track of adverse reactions other than death. Can you imagine if there was some other operation or procedure where they didn't keep track of serious side effects and botched procedures?

One of the biggest risks of chemical abortion is that a woman could be experiencing an ectopic pregnancy, in which a baby is growing outside of the womb. This can and has been deadly for women, but this is of no concern to the abortion lobby. During the months that many states were locked down because of the COVID-19 pandemic, the FDA relaxed its rules on chemical abortion and allowed women to receive prescriptions through the mail, without ever seeing a doctor. This greatly increases the likelihood that a woman experiencing an ectopic pregnancy will not know it—possibly until it's too late.

Abortions Past Ten Weeks

Once a woman reaches ten weeks since her last menstrual period, chemical abortion is no longer an option. Instead, she will have to go to an abortion business or doctor for a first trimester suction abortion. This is still the most common technique for women until their twelfth week.

In this procedure, a thin tube called a cannula is attached to a bottle and a pump. The pump acts like a vacuum to suction the baby from the womb, collecting the baby's blood and body parts. It's a quick procedure, but if performed without any kind of anesthesia—as it often is—it hurts. The

---

failure%3B%E2%80%9D%20thrombotic%20thrombocytopenic.

dangers of this kind of abortion include uncontrolled bleeding afterward, or tears to the uterus or cervix. Ordinarily, there is a person in each abortion business whose job it is to sift through the parts of the baby to make sure nothing has been left inside the mom. If any of these "products of conception" (there's another euphemism) are left in a woman's womb, she will need a second abortion to remove them. Leaving them there will cause infection and can even lead to death.

After the abortion, women are usually shown to a recovery room with other women who have also just had abortions. Women from Silent No More have described this part of the procedure as the saddest part, because they know there is no going back. Their babies are dead. Women sit in recliners, each enveloped in her own sadness, until staffers tell them to get dressed and leave.

Different states have different laws surrounding abortion. In some states, moms have to have an ultrasound before the abortion; some make women wait twenty-four or even seventy-two hours between the time they make the appointment and when the abortion actually takes place. Some states require minors to tell at least one parent about the abortion, and some require consent of the parent, unless the girl goes before a family court judge.

In states with few or no abortion restrictions, school officials can actually help a girl leave class, have an abortion, and go home in the afternoon as though nothing has happened. If that same girl was having an attack of appendicitis, which can be deadly, her parents would have to be notified and give consent before a surgeon could remove her appendix.

Once a woman enters her thirteenth week of pregnancy, she is in her second trimester. Things become even riskier here. An abortion at this stage is called D&E, which stands for dilation and evacuation. In pro-life circles, we call this a dismemberment abortion because the child in the womb is literally pulled apart. The abortionist uses forceps to enter a woman's womb again and again, each time grasping whatever he can and then pulling it out. The baby's head is usually the last thing to come out and often it has to be crushed before it can be pulled through the mother's birth canal.

Most of the women who have died from abortion in recent years have been victims of botched second-trimester abortions. Most of them are women of color whose deteriorating conditions were overlooked or ignored by the staff at the abortion mill. There was a case in the news about a woman named Tonya Reaves who died in 2012. She had undergone three abortion procedures and been left bleeding for several hours at Planned Parenthood before being transferred to a hospital.[6] In 2014, Lakisha Wilson had a second-trimester abortion, during which she suffered uncontrolled bleeding and stopped breathing. When 911 was called, paramedics had to climb the stairs to third-floor treatment room because the elevator in the Cleveland abortion mill was broken. When they reached her, she had not taken a breath for twenty-five minutes. She died a week later.[7]

---

[6]   Janet Morana, "Questions still linger five years after Tonya Reaves was killed by abortion," *Daily Caller*, July 20, 2017, https://dailycaller.com /2017/07/20/questions-still-linger-five-years-after-tonya-reaves-was-kil led-by-abortion/.

[7]   Cheryl Sullenger, "Why Lakisha Wilson died after an abortion at

Abortion is not safe, and it is not health care. But it is legal even through the third trimester.

These very late abortions can take two, three, or even four days. Most of them begin with the abortionist injecting a substance into the baby that will stop his or her heart. Then little rods of seaweed called laminaria are inserted in the mother's cervix to begin to open it up. This process goes on for as long as it takes for the cervix to be open enough for the mom to give birth to her stillborn baby.

The abortion lobby and its friends in the mainstream media say these very late abortions are rare and only take place if the mother's life is in jeopardy or if the baby was going to die anyway. These are lies.

At Priests for Life, we work with an attorney from Albuquerque, New Mexico who has obtained records from a late-term abortion business there. These records show women scheduling abortion appointments at twenty-four, twenty-eight, or even thirty-two weeks, and we did our own undercover phone calls to that same business. Our caller was able to schedule an abortion at thirty weeks, with the staffer on the phone most interested in how the mother was going to pay for this very expensive abortion procedure.

Several years ago, we were contacted by the family of a young woman from Great Britain who was headed to New Mexico to abort her baby at thirty weeks. Her mother, uncle, and other relatives were desperate to stop her, but her father, who accompanied his healthy daughter and healthy

---

Preterm in Cleveland," *Operation Rescue*, March 5, 2015, https://www .operationrescue.org/archives/npr-ignores-facts-about-ohio-abortion-pa tient-death-while-siding-with-those-that-killed-her/.

grandchild, saw to it that she went through with the abortion. Healthy mother, healthy baby.

A Sad Story about Madison

Here is yet another story of a very late-term abortion that broke our hearts at Priests for Life. The couple involved lived in Westchester County, New York. Being from New York myself, I took a special interest in this story.

In 2013, Jennifer Morbelli, a twenty-nine-year-old substitute kindergarten teacher, and her husband were looking forward to the birth of their daughter, Madison. Yes, they had named her and had her room all ready. Friends could select gifts from a baby registry. But at her doctor's appointment at thirty-two weeks, the couple was told their daughter would be born with a seizure disorder. The couple, probably on the advice of a doctor, chose to have an abortion.

At that time, abortion in New York was legal until the twenty-fourth week of pregnancy (after the passage of a new law in 2019, it is now legal in the state to abort a baby through the ninth month). Jennifer was referred to late-term abortionist LeRoy Carhart and his killing center in Maryland, Germantown Reproductive Health Services.

Jennifer and her family arrived at Carhart's abortion mill on Sunday, February 3. Madison was now at thirty-three weeks gestation. The first step in the abortion, as I mentioned before, was to have a lethal injection shot through the heart of the unborn baby girl. This would kill Madison.

Jennifer returned to Carhart on Monday to begin the process of having her cervix dilated. The plan was to have her deliver her dead baby on Wednesday, so she had to return Tuesday to continue the dilation process. Pro-lifers outside the killing center who saw Jennifer on Wednesday were quoted as saying she looked weak. After nine hours in the abortion mill, she returned to the hotel. Madison, dead already for two days, had been delivered.

Early the next morning, Jennifer began to experience chest pains. The family tried repeatedly to reach Dr. Carhart, but he had already left the state, so they drove Jennifer to Shady Grove Adventist Hospital in Rockville, Maryland. At 9:30 a.m., the family was informed that Jennifer had died.

The Maryland Office of the Chief Medical Examiner ruled that Jennifer died from "disseminated intravascular coagulation," "due to or as a consequence of amniotic fluid embolism following medical termination of pregnancy."[8] This means that amniotic fluid in her womb spilled into her bloodstream, causing widespread blood clots.

The obituary in Jennifer's hometown newspaper said "Jennifer McKenna-Morbelli of New Rochelle, passed away suddenly on Thursday February 7, 2013 at age 29 with her baby girl Madison Leigh."[9]

The abortion designed to kill Madison also claimed her mother's life. They were buried together at a cemetery in Rye, New York.

---

[8]   Maryland Department of Health and Mental Hygiene, death certificate 201306084, Jennifer Morbelli, digital image, accessed November 15, 2021, http://operationrescue.org/pdfs/MorbelliDeath Certificate-Redacted.pdf.

[9]   "Obituary," Jennifer Leigh McKenna Morbelli, died February 7, 2013, Find a Grave, accessed November 15, 2021, https://www .findagrave.com/memorial/105045569/jennifer-leigh-morbelli.

Unfortunately, Jennifer Morbelli's story in not unique. Doctors in this country are only too quick to recommend termination when there is anything wrong with the unborn child. But dire circumstances are not needed to kill a viable, nearly full-term baby in this country. Anyone who tells you something different is lying.

There were parts of this chapter that were no doubt difficult to read. But we must know the truth behind this barbaric practice. We cannot sugarcoat it like the abortion industry does.

Now, with this behind us, let's approach a different side of the story. Many people say they are against abortion in general—they know it is a horrible procedure like the one described in this chapter—but they still think it should be legal in certain unfortunate situations. It's time to discuss why nothing can justify the killing of an unborn child.

6

A Pro-Life Defense against Special Circumstance Abortions

"What about the Difficult Cases?"

Whenever there is a discussion about ending or restricting abortion, someone will raise the question "What about the difficult cases?" They are referring to incidents of rape and incest that result in pregnancy, when a baby in the womb has been diagnosed with a serious illness or a disorder like Down syndrome, or when the life of the mother is endangered by the pregnancy.

Let's look at each of these individually.

Cases of Rape and Incest

Many people who would otherwise call themselves pro-life believe women who are victims of rape deserve the right to terminate the lives of their unborn children. Short of murder, rape is the worst physical and emotional assault against women. In 2019, the last year for which statistics are available, 459,310 women and girls in the United States were raped,[1] most of them between the ages of twelve and thirty-four.[2]

Abortion does not erase the rape, *it merely responds to one evil with another.* Rape is a grave injustice, but so is killing an innocent child. Rape victims who become pregnant might choose abortion because they can't bear the thought of giving birth to their attacker's child. But far from freeing a rape victim from their physical and psychological scars, abortion brings with it its own set of sufferings, damages, and regrets.

No one has completely reliable numbers on the percentage of abortions performed because of rape or incest, because not all of these rapes—incest is often rape as well—are reported, and women might not reveal to an abortionist that rape is the reason they're aborting. But the generally accepted number is that 1 percent of abortions are performed on women who conceived through rape, and .005 percent on incest victims. It is important to remember this statistic when someone says abortion should be legal just because of these cases. This is a dodge of the issue by trying to present extremely rare and heartbreaking cases. More often than not, when people bring up these sorts of cases, like rape, they are trying to gloss over and ignore the other 99 percent of cases. They're trying to look for a way to justify their position by painting the other side as unsympathetic to rape victims, which is grossly unfair. The facts show these cases are a very

---

[1]   Jenifer Kuadli, "32 Shocking Sexual Assault Statistics for 2021," Legal Jobs, January 24, 2021, https://legaljobs.io/blog/sexual-assault-statistics/.

[2]   "Criminal Victimization, 2019," Department of Justice, September 2020, https://bjs.ojp.gov/content/pub/pdf/cv19.pdf.

slim minority of abortions. In any debate (not just this one) we cannot pull out rare cases to make decisions for the rest of the population.

Furthermore, when we talk about keeping abortion legal because rape victims need that option, we are sacrificing the other 99 percent of babies aborted. I'm sure that seems unfair, but something else that's unfair is the insistence that these 1 percenters have no right to life. An organization called Save the 1 gives a voice to people whose fathers were rapists and whose mothers chose life anyway. These survivors make a very good point: their right to life is as absolute as anyone else's.

There is also the false presumption that an abortion will take away the pain of being sexually assaulted. In fact, the opposite is usually true.

Dr. David Reardon of the Elliott Institute has done extensive research on the effects of abortion on women. His book *Victims and Victors* grew out of a study he did on women who became pregnant through sexual assault.[3]

Of 192 women who became pregnant as a result of rape or incest, 164 were victims of rape and 28 were victims of incest. Overall, 69 percent continued the pregnancy and either raised the child or made an adoption plan, 29 percent had abortions, and 1.5 percent had miscarriages. Here are some of Dr. Reardon's findings:

---

[3]   David C. Reardon, Julie Makimaa, and Amy Sobie, eds., *Victims and Victors: Speaking Out About their Pregnancies, Abortions and Children Conceived in Sexual Assault* (Acorn Books, 2000).

- Nearly 80 percent of the women who aborted the pregnancy reported that abortion had been the wrong solution.
- Most women who had abortions said abortion only increased the trauma they were experiencing.
- In many cases, the victim faced strong pressure or demands to abort. Forty-three percent of rape victims who aborted said they felt pressured or were strongly directed by family members or health workers to abort.
- In almost every case where an incest victim had an abortion, her parents or someone else made the decision to abort for her. In several cases, the abortion was carried out against her wishes, and in a few cases, without her knowledge that she was pregnant or that an abortion was taking place.
- None of the women who gave birth to a child conceived in sexual assault expressed regret or wished they had aborted instead.

One woman, Edith, was impregnated by her stepfather at the age of twelve. Her mother, who knew of the abuse, took her for an abortion. Years later, Edith wrote, "Throughout the years I have been depressed, suicidal, furious, outraged, lonely, and have felt a sense of loss. . . . The abortion which was to 'be in my best interest' just has not been. As far as I can tell, it only 'saved their reputations,' 'solved their problems,' and allowed their lives to go merrily on. . . . Problems are not ended by abortion, but only made worse."[4]

---

[4]   Ibid.

Another woman from the Reardon study, Kathleen DeZeeuw, raised her son after experiencing a date rape as a teen. She wrote that she believed abortion advocates have exploited stories like hers: "Having lived through rape, and also having raised a child conceived in rape, I feel personally assaulted and insulted every time I hear that abortion should be legal because of rape and incest. I feel that we're being used to further the abortion issue, even though we've not been asked to tell our side of the story."[5]

The Silent No More Awareness Campaign does ask women to tell their side of the story. Here are some of those experiences.[6]

Christina from Alberta, Canada, writes:[7]

> I had an abortion because I was a seventeen-year-old drug addict who was raped. I hid the pregnancy for months and once my mother found out, she promptly made it clear to me that I would not be "keeping it." I was so far along that I had a partial-birth abortion. Of course, they did not tell me this salient fact. During the abortion I experienced pain like I've never felt before and I could feel my little baby crying out for help. She did not want to die. I began to scream and cry, but to no avail. The nurse . . . told me to be quiet. My three-day abortion was complete. Immediately

---

5   Ibid.
6   The following testimonials come from the Silent No More Awareness Campaign, https://www.silentnomoreawareness.org/testimo nies/index.aspx.
7   This story and others in this chapter may be difficult for some to read.

after the abortion I felt dead inside. I awoke weeping, bleeding profusely, and in the fetal position in a room filled with other women who were all doing the same thing. I began to abuse drugs that I had never touched before. I did quite a bit of damage to myself. As time went on I felt angry, depressed, and hopeless. I began to obsess about my terrible deed, and felt I would surely go to hell for what I had done.

Christina suffered trauma as a result of her rape, but she also suffered from the trauma of ending the life of her unborn child. Abortion did not make her pain go away; it added new sufferings and more anguish.

Nicole from Virginia also writes about how her abortion served only to make the trauma of her rape worse:

I deeply regret the abortion I had four weeks after being raped. There is no good reason to have an abortion. All the logical reasons fail to keep your heart from breaking when it's over. If, like me, you were raped, and you think you can't bear nine months of pregnancy, I can tell you from experience the seventeen years of regret have been worse. I realized too late that my baby was a gift from a loving God who wanted to give me a purpose for my pain. . . . The abortion was the beginning of the real nightmare for me. . . . The abortion made healing from rape infinitely more difficult by compounding the trauma. . . . Abortion is not the answer for rape.

What about women who were raped and decided to give birth? How did they feel? Were they reminded of the rape during the pregnancy? Did looking at their child make them think of the rapist? What about children conceived as a result of rape? How do they feel when later they find out about their conception?

Liz was a seventeen-year-old pro-life high school student in Kentucky who was drugged and date raped after a party during her senior year: "I would never have told anyone about it, except I got pregnant." She knew the rape was not her fault, and she wanted "an easy fix." Even though she had always been pro-life, she was planning to have an abortion until a friend said to her, "You know you can't kill a baby."

Through Catholic Social Services, Liz arranged an open adoption for the little boy. People often ask her if she sees the face of her attacker when she looks at her son, this boy who is being raised in a loving home. Her answer: "I have never seen anything other than that beautiful boy."

This story is not unique to Liz.

Juda's mother was walking home from a movie theater in St. Louis when she was raped by several men. When she learned she was pregnant, she decided to offer the gift of life to her blameless child and to make an adoption plan for her. Decades later, after learning the circumstances of her birth and adoption, Juda met her courageous birth mother. "It was the most wonderful reunion," she recalled. "She's a hero."

Although Juda was already pro-life, the knowledge that she was conceived in rape energized her pro-life activism. Juda has spoken at Harvard University, and both she and her mother have shared their story on television. Both have forgiven the rapists.

Juda knows her mother was empowered by refusing to have an abortion. She went on to marry and have two more children. Now she's a grandmother. To those pro-lifers who still believe abortion should remain legal for rape victims, Juda says, "I am not the exception."

As we have shown through the testimonies of those conceived in rape and those who have become pregnant by rape, abortion does nothing to erase the violence, fear, and trauma of the experience. In fact, for many women, abortion adds to their suffering.

What If the Baby Is Sick or Handicapped?

When a baby in the womb is diagnosed with a life-threatening or life-limiting disorder, many doctors—and well-meaning friends and relatives—will recommend termination, also known as abortion. But is abortion a helpful solution in these cases? Let's look a little closer.

Several tests are performed during pregnancy to monitor the well-being of the unborn child. During the first trimester, these include routine blood tests and sonograms. The number of sonograms depends upon the doctor. My daughter had a sonogram on every visit to her OB/GYN, every three weeks during the first and second trimester, and every week in the last trimester. Also at twelve weeks, there is a blood test to rule out cystic fibrosis.

In the second trimester, between the fifteenth and seventeenth weeks, most pregnant women have an alpha-fetoprotein (AFP) screening, a blood test that measures a

Meet the Unborn Child!

I am an Embryo!

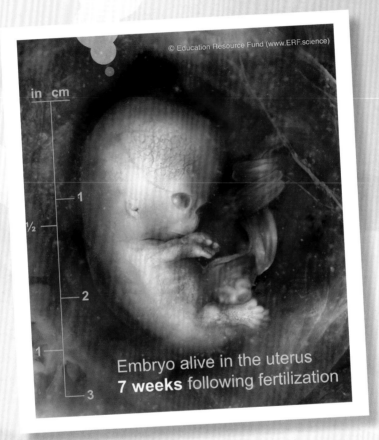

© Education Resource Fund (www.ERF.science)

in cm

Embryo alive in the uterus
7 weeks following fertilization

7 Weeks

At this point, I am still, in scientific terms, an "embryo."

From 7 to 7½ weeks, my tendons attach leg muscles to bones, and knee joints appear.

By 7½ weeks, my hands can be brought together, as can my feet. I can kick, and will jump if startled.

By 7 to 7½ weeks, my nephrons, the basic filtration units in my kidneys, begin to form.

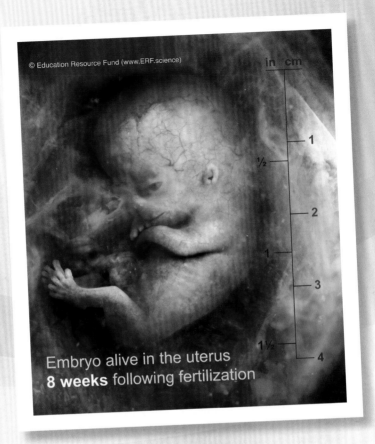

in cm

Embryo alive in the uterus
8 weeks following fertilization

8 Weeks

Once I've completed 8 weeks of development, I'm now considered a "fetus."

My heart has already beaten over 7 million times. My heart began to beat 3 weeks and 1 day following fertilization.

I am now the size of a cherry tomato, have more than 4,000 body parts routinely found in newborns and adults, and possess about 1 billion specialized cells, forming nearly all components of all body systems!

I am beginning to perform occasional breathing motions.

My eyelids have begun to fuse together and completely cover my eyes.

I am now a Fetus!

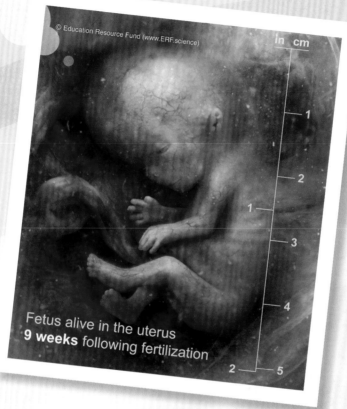

© Education Resource Fund (www.ERF.science)

in cm

Fetus alive in the uterus
9 weeks following fertilization

9 Weeks

I am now the size of a small tomato.

My face, palms of my hands, and soles of my feet now sense and respond to light touch.

My mouth opens and closes, and my tongue moves.

I am now swallowing amniotic fluid.

I can sigh, stretch, and move my head.

As a baby girl, I have early reproductive cells in my ovaries.

I have begun sucking my thumb.

I have begun grasping objects.

If touched near my mouth, my face now turns toward the side touched.

I have begun to yawn.

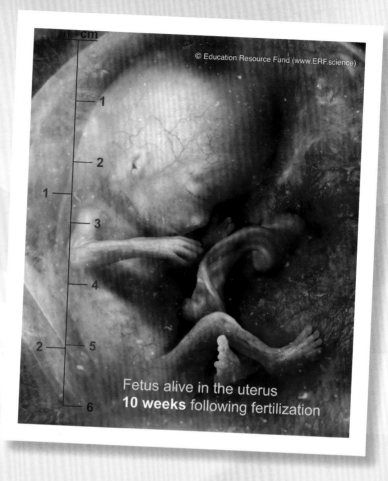

Fetus alive in the uterus
10 weeks following fertilization

10 Weeks

I am now the size of a purple-top turnip.

My body weight has increased more than 75% just this week.

My bones are hardening throughout my body.

My fingernails and toenails have begun to grow.

The right and left sides of my brain are connecting.

My unique fingerprints have begun forming.

Lightly touching one of my upper eyelids causes both eyes to roll downward.

Here I am at 12 weeks!

12 Weeks

One day I'm going to be out there running and playing!

I'm 3 months old now!

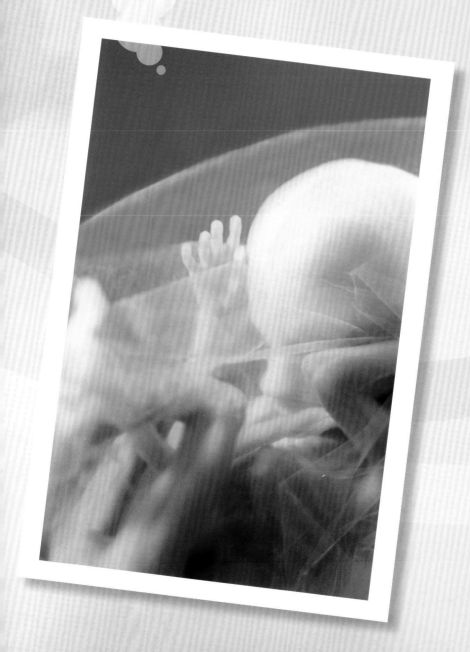

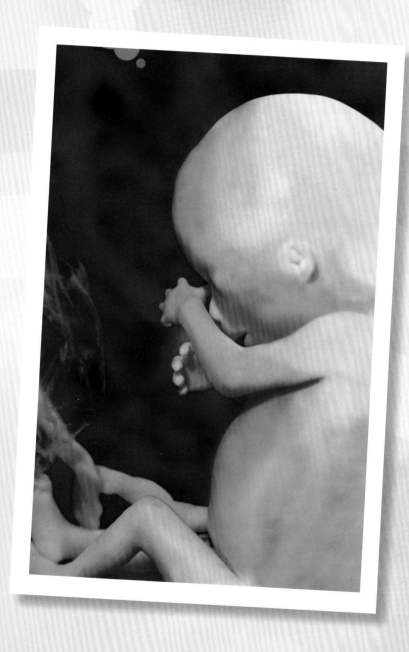

4 Months

Look at me, I can open my mouth to yawn!

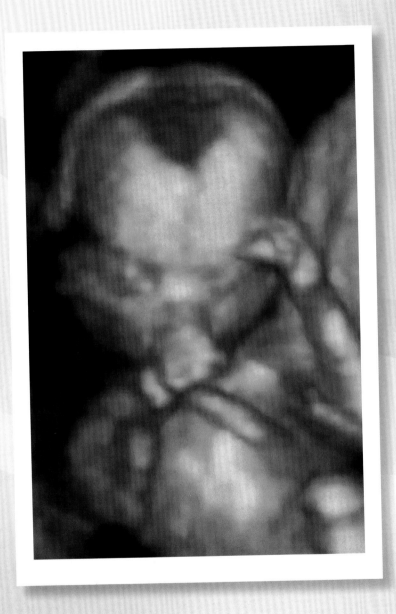

4 Months

I like to relax and suck my thumb!

I'm 5 months old now!

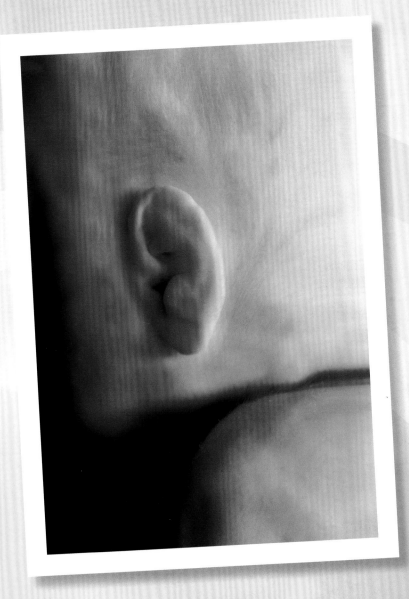

5 Months

I love listening to my mommy and daddy talk.
Especially when they read and sing to me.

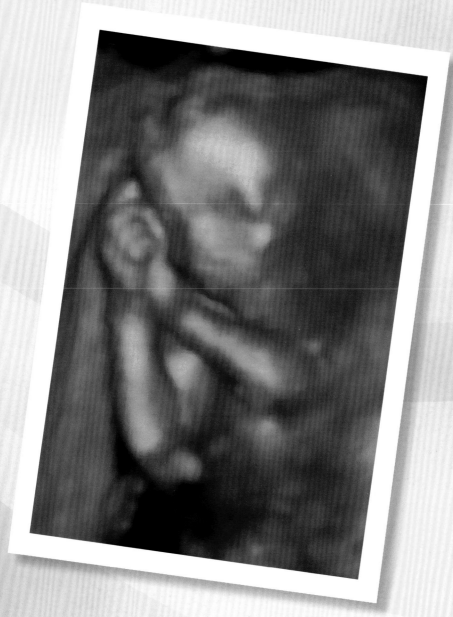

5 Months

Look at me, I can clap my hands now!

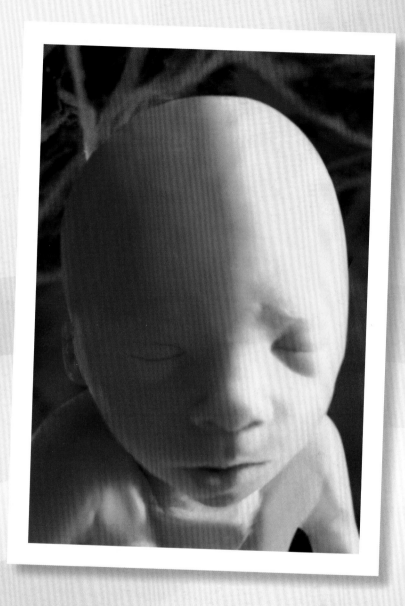

6 Months

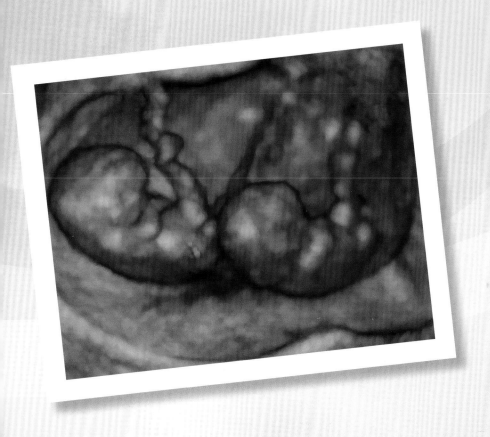

Twins!

We love kicking mommy together!

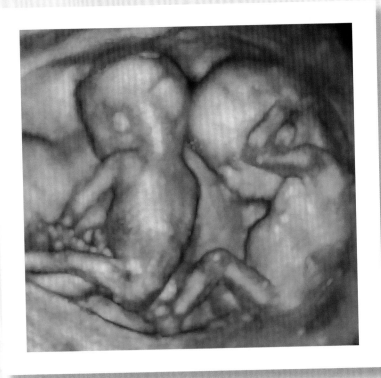

Twins!

It's getting crowded in here.
Can't wait until it's time to come out
and meet mommy and daddy.

These images are 3D and 4D ultrasound provided by Soundwave Images, Shari Richard, www.unborn.com

Priests for Life is grateful to Professor Andrzej Skawina (Collegium Medicum Jagiellonian University, Krakow) and Dr. Antoni Marsinek, MD (Czerwiakowski Gynecological and Obstetrics Hospital, Krakow) for making the developing baby images above (beginning at 12 weeks) available, and to the Zrodlo Foundation, Wychowawca Department, for the permission to use them.

protein normally produced by the baby's liver. Abnormal levels of AFP could mean the baby will be born with spina bifida, neural tube defects, Down syndrome, or other chromosomal abnormalities or defects. The test also can indicate twins or a miscalculated due date. The AFP test, which is notorious for providing false positives, is an indication that further, more invasive testing is needed.

If a woman is older than thirty-five, amniocentesis or chorionic villus sampling is recommended to look for fetal anomalies. With many OB/GYNs, once a patient has a diagnosis of a fetal anomaly, termination of the pregnancy is discussed, and in some cases, strongly advised. Let's look at some people who have had these experiences.

Laura Cuimei[8] was pregnant with her second child when her doctor sent her for an AFP test early in her second trimester. She and her husband, Curt, were stunned when the results came back.

"They said I probably was carrying a Down syndrome baby," the New Jersey resident recalled. "I was only twenty-seven at the time, and we never expected something like that."

Her doctor was Catholic, working in a Catholic hospital, so he did not outright suggest that the couple consider abortion. But he did drop hints, Laura said. The doctor did recommend amniocentesis, a prenatal diagnostic test in which a long needle is inserted through a woman's stomach into the womb to draw up some of the amniotic fluid surrounding the baby. The procedure, although not very painful to the mother, carries a significant risk of miscarriage. The Cuimeis

---

[8]   Laura's story comes from a personal conversation with the author.

declined. "We knew that whether the baby had Down syndrome or not, we would love the baby."

A sonogram done a few weeks later indicated the baby was fine, but the worry "was never far from my mind." A full-term, healthy baby was born, and the couple named him Christopher.

While Laura and her husband would not have aborted their Down syndrome baby, the truth is that many couples do. A recent survey of studies done on Down syndrome and abortion found that the population of those with the disorder has been reduced by 30 percent since 1974.[9]

What about those couples who went with a doctor's advice to terminate the pregnancy? How did they feel afterward? Nancy Kreuzer from Illinois tells her story.

> My baby was 22 weeks, I was five and a half months pregnant, when I was told that she had water on the brain (hydrocephalus) and was advised by my doctor to "terminate the pregnancy." It was explained that the abortion would be a simple procedure. My husband and I were told we could leave this behind us, get on with our lives and try for another baby.
>
> Because I was in my second trimester of pregnancy, the abortion was a two-day procedure. It was not, as the doctor described, "simple." At the abortion clinic no one asked how I was or explained what was happening

---

[9]   Gert de Graaf, Frank F. Buckley, Brian G. Skotko, "Estimates of the live births, natural losses, and elective terminations with down syndrome in the United States," Am J Med Genet Part A 167A (2015):756–67.

to me. I felt alone, afraid and devastated. While I sat, waiting for the doctor to arrive, many nurses and workers in the abortion clinic casually walked by me. I sat there for hours. Tears streamed down my face but no one talked to me, no one acknowledged my pain.

The day after my abortion, I felt numb. I left the abortion clinic with no baby to bury, no doll-size casket, no funeral service, no grave to adorn with flowers. I vomited in the parking lot and rode home in silence. No one brought meals, no one sent cards, no one called, because I had been too ashamed to tell anyone what I had agreed to. In the weeks to follow, I tried to bury the memory of the abortion and not look back.

In the months and years afterward, there were clear signs that the scars of my abortion existed, but I didn't recognize them at the time. Interestingly, I assumed I was doing just fine. But below the surface, I was unusually fearful. As time went on, I often had the sense that I wanted to run and I had repeated nightmares of running from something horrible. I would awaken panicked, unable to sleep the rest of the night. There was an internal sadness, not visible to the world.[10]

Despite children with Down syndrome and other handicaps not being in danger of death from their condition, it is insinuated that you are doing them a favor by killing them in the womb so that they don't have to live a "handicapped" life.

---

[10] Nancy Kreuzer, "Never Alone," Silent No More Awareness Campaign, accessed November 30, 2021, https://www.silentnomoreawareness.org/testimonies/testimony.aspx?ID=2323.

But who are we to determine when someone gets to live and die? We are not God. Could you ever imagine walking up to a five-year-old, a ten-year-old, a twenty-year-old individual with a handicap and killing them, thinking you are doing them a favor? It is impossible to even think of it. Why, then, would we think it is okay to terminate them in the womb?

But what about when a couple learns their child has an illness that will end his or her life days or minutes after birth? What are their options? Isn't this different? Because abortion is legal all through pregnancy, couples often choose to abort these late-term babies because they feel they have no other choice. But they do.

"We've always been taught in OB-GYN that we have two patients, that there are two lives there," said Dr. Mary Davenport, a pro-life physician.[11] "But now people are told really ridiculous things about needing to abort their babies that are not even true."

Both Dr. Davenport and Dr. John Bruchalski, a pro-life physician who did abortions early in his career, said doctors who are already paying high malpractice insurance are afraid of being sued for "wrongful birth" if babies are born with abnormalities.

"Ninety-five percent of all doctors in the US will recommend abortion if babies are found to have any of a growing list of diseases or disorders," Dr. Bruchalski claims. "We have become eugenicists[12] overnight."[13]

---

[11]   Mary Davenport, interview with author.
[12]   A eugenicist is someone who believes the human race can be improved by breeding out people with certain diseases or disabilities.
[13]   John Bruchalski, interview with author.

Dr. Davenport said doctors insist on prenatal testing under the guise of giving their patients time to prepare for the challenges of dealing with a sick child. But that's a ruse. "They can be liable for a lot of money. That's the bottom line. It's given so many doctors a eugenic orientation."

Birth defects once were considered unexpected setbacks, challenges for parents who assumed they would be coming home from the hospital with a perfect baby girl or boy. But in our abortion-friendly, lawsuit-happy society, doctors who work in reproductive medicine now can find themselves named in "wrongful birth" or "wrongful life" lawsuits.

A wrongful birth suit is brought by parents who say they would have aborted had they known their baby would be born with a serious illness. Wrongful life, recognized only in a few states (California, New Jersey, and Washington), are brought on behalf of an infant and claims it would have been better had he or she never been born. I'm sure many of you have heard someone say—or maybe you said it yourself—"I wish I had never been born." But does anyone really mean that?

There are alternatives to abortion and wrongful life suits. "We had to have something to offer people other than 'don't do that,'" Dr. Byron Calhoun said of late-term abortions.[14] That something is perinatal hospice, which Dr. Calhoun helped pioneer.

Parents are able to plan for the birth with the support of doctors, nurses, counselors, clergy, and family. Babies are bathed, dressed, cuddled, and surrounded by the love every

---

[14]   Byron Calhoun, interview with author.

baby deserves, and should they die from their condition, it is with the dignity every human being deserves. Parents who choose perinatal hospice still have to deal with the grief that comes from losing a child, but studies have shown they can deal with that grief much better than women who choose late-term abortion.

"We explain that they're not going to escape any of the grief, but we ask them if they want to spend time with their babies," Dr. Calhoun said, adding that 75 percent of couples choose perinatal hospice when it's offered.

For those who are able to nurture and cherish their infants, "there's grief and there's sadness," Dr. Calhoun said, "but there's no post-traumatic stress."

Baby Gianna

A personal story always helps things hit home.

Andrew Smith used to work for Priests for Life when our office was located in New York City. Years later, he and his wife, Jacquelyn, were pregnant with their seventh child when they were told the baby had trisomy 18. Abortion was suggested. I interviewed the Smiths for a story for the *National Catholic Register*. The following is excerpted from that story:

> Jacquelyn politely told the doctor, "Ma'am, in this family we deliver our babies."
>
> Her husband was less diplomatic.
>
> "We don't kill our babies," Andrew said.
>
> Trisomy 18 is a rare genetic disorder characterized by three copies of chromosome 18 instead of two. Many babies with the disorder die before they are

born. Others die during the birth process or shortly after. The unluckiest among them are aborted or have care withheld at birth. A few survive and thrive.

The Smiths are devout Catholics and passionately pro-life—Jacquelyn is the Youth for Life Director for the Respect Life Ministry in the Diocese of Dallas—so they knew they had options other than abortion or comfort care. But parents who find themselves at the mercy of our throwaway culture might be led to believe abortion is their only choice.

"The pro-abortion medical community takes that moment of being scared and says, 'Act now. Terminate,'" Jacquelyn said. "I was planning on a healthy baby, and I wasn't going to have a healthy baby. It was hard and I had to process that. Then I had to prepare for the baby I was having."

When the Smiths found out the baby was a girl, they chose the name Gemma Gianna Perpetua Smith, a name honoring St. Gianna Molla, who gave up her life for her unborn child and who has been named one of the patrons of pregnant women.

"From the beginning, we celebrated Gemma as a member of our family," Jacquelyn said.

The Smiths got in touch with an organization called Be Not Afraid, a Catholic nonprofit that works with parents whose babies have received life-limiting diagnoses, including Trisomy 18.

The Smiths and their advocates at Be Not Afraid worked out a birth plan for Gemma that included every eventuality, including heart surgery at the

Children's Medical Center in Dallas if Gemma was up to it.

That plan turned out not to be.

Jacquelyn's doctors determined that a cesarean section delivery was the safest for Gemma. It was scheduled for February 4. But after an ultrasound on January 31, the Smiths were sent to the hospital.

Gemma was born at 2:30 p.m. Andrew baptized her immediately and then she was taken to the neonatal intensive care unit.

Her kidneys and one of her lungs were not functioning. Her overall heart function was not what it should be. Andrew raced home to get the rest of the children. The hospital had agreed to let them all in if death appeared imminent (although there was some last-minute resistance from the staff). A family picture was finally taken at midnight.

"I was the first to hold her," Jacquelyn said, but eventually all of Gemma's siblings had their moment with their baby sister.

Father Christopher Andrew of St. Basil the Great Byzantine Catholic Church confirmed Gemma in the faith and gave her First Communion, placing drops of consecrated wine on her tongue and giving the rest to Jacquelyn. Draped in a white gown provided by Be Not Afraid, Gemma was also given the Sacrament of Anointing of the Sick.

Gemma was then hooked up to a ventilator. This kept the family from knowing the exact moment she passed, but they are thankful that her 28 hours

were filled with love, care, and the sacraments of the
Church.

Jacquelyn said her advice to other moms facing a
serious prenatal diagnosis would be never to give up
hope.

"Until the child is born, you can't know what the
medical challenges are," she said. "Enjoy the time you
have her in your belly. Research like crazy. And be
ready to be a mama bear."[15]

There are alternatives and help for parents facing a pregnancy with a fatal or abnormal diagnosis. Organizations like
Be Not Afraid and Prenatal Partners for Life are dedicated to
providing families—those who have or are expecting a special-needs child—the support, information, and encouragement they need to make informed decisions involving their
preborn or newborn child's care. They believe these children
are unique gifts from God and have a special purpose in life
that only they can fulfill. Their goal is to provide honest,
practical information about parenting a special-needs child
by linking expectant parents or new parents with those who
are already caring for these cherished children.[16]

---

[15]   Janet Morana, "28 Hours Filled With Love and Eternity Filed
        With Joy," *National Catholic Register*, May 20, 2020, https://www
        .ncregister.com/blog/28-hours-filled-with-love-and-eternity-filled
        -with-joy.

[16]   Visit www.prenatalpartnersforlife.org and BeNotAfraid.net to
        learn more about these organizations, and get more information
        about perinatal hospice at www.perinatalhospice.org.

The Health of the Mother

One of the most misunderstood issues in the abortion debate is the position of the Catholic Church when it comes to a pregnancy that endangers the life of the mother.

According to the teachings of our Church, a doctor cannot abort a child to save the mother. But if the child dies during a lifesaving procedure or treatment for the mother, the unborn baby's death is an unfortunate but unavoidable side effect. To try to save them both, doctors, including Dr. Byron Calhoun in West Virginia, will allow the pregnancy to progress as long as possible without jeopardizing the mother, then deliver the baby and do everything possible to keep the child alive.

"It's always wrong to directly kill an innocent human being, regardless of their stage of life," said Dr. John Haas, president of the National Catholic Bioethics Center in Philadelphia. "If you make a list of exceptions, where does it stop? There's no logical place to draw that line. All human life is sacred, and has to be sacred."[17]

Pro-life physicians like Dr. Bruchalski agree.

"You never pit the life of the mother against the life of the child. You have to have a relationship with the patient to be able to convince her that you won't let her die and that her baby doesn't have to die either. What we do with mothers at risk is practice good medicine. We monitor her, in the hospital or even in intensive care if we need to. We deliver the baby when we have to."[18]

---

[17]   John Haas, interview with author.
[18]   John Bruchalski, interview with author.

Many doctors will recommend abortion for women suffering from drug addiction, heart disease, or other complications. For these women, Dr. Bruchalski said it might become necessary to deliver their babies before they are viable, leaving those babies with a high probability of death. But delivering a baby is a far cry from aborting a baby, as the American Association of Pro-Life Obstetrician Gynecologists (AAPLOG) notes in its official policy statement:

> Abortion is the purposeful killing of the unborn in the termination of a pregnancy. AAPLOG opposes abortion. When extreme medical emergencies that threaten the life of the mother arise . . AAPLOG believes in "treatment to save the mother's life," including premature delivery if that is indicated—obviously with the patient's informed consent. This is NOT "abortion to save the mother's life." We are treating two patients, the mother and the baby, and every reasonable attempt to save the baby's life would also be a part of our medical intervention. We acknowledge that, in some such instances, the baby would be too premature to survive.[19]

Dr. Calhoun said doctors "just need to be doctors. Control the diabetes. Control the hypertension. Treat your patient. You don't have to kill the baby. It's a ridiculous argument to justify killing a baby."

---

[19]   "What is AAPLOG's Position on 'Abortion to Save the Life of the Mother?'" American Association of Pro-Life Obstetrician Gynecologists, July 2009, https://aaplog.org/what-is-aaplogs-position-on-abortion-to-save -the-life-of-the-mother/.

A baby at twenty-four weeks gestation is considered "viable" or able to survive outside the womb with medical help. But babies are surviving even earlier than that now. One little girl who was born at twenty-one weeks in Great Britain celebrated her first birthday as I wrote this book.

The longer the baby stays in the womb, of course, the greater the chances he or she will survive. About 50 percent of babies born in the twenty-fourth week will make it. That rate goes up to 90 percent for babies who can stay in the womb until twenty-eight weeks.[20]

Women who take their doctors' advice to abort their children can suffer severe emotional effects.

Here's the story of one woman who took her doctor's advice and ended the life of her unborn child because she was led to believe her life was in jeopardy. Cheryl from California was born with a defective valve in her heart and it played a role in the birth of her first child:

> After I gave birth to my daughter Stephanie, I could not breathe but the heart doctor thought I would make it. When I got pregnant again, I was so weak I could not care for my other two children. By now I knew the Lord well but my faith left me and fear haunted my every step.
>
> Everyone I spoke to said that I had two other children to care for and it was all right if I chose my life

---

[20] "When Is It Safe to Deliver Your Baby?" University of Utah, accessed November 16, 2021, https://healthcare.utah.edu/womens health/pregnancy-birth/preterm-birth/when-is-it-safe-to-deliver .php.

over the life of my unborn baby. Oh this haunted me. I just wanted to die. What kind of mother puts her life before that of her unborn child? No one that I spoke with ever counseled me. It took me years to forgive myself. Now I realized I was not more important than my unborn child.[21]

Cheryl's experience confirms what many other women have said in their Silent No More testimonies: Having an abortion can leave lifelong psychological scars. A mother's maternal instinct is to save her child. What mother on a sinking ship would not put the life vest on her children first? If a car was careening out of control, wouldn't every mother push the baby carriage out of the way first, even if that meant she might be hit by a car?

Choosing life is always the right choice, even when it's hard, even when it's scary, even when the outcome is unclear. And given advances in medicine in the past decades, the so-called choice between baby and mother is becoming increasingly rare, even to the point that it is practically non-existent (this is another rare case people will bring up when they are just trying to justify the killing of so many babies during "regular" abortions).

Those who advocate for abortion often fall back on the example of ectopic pregnancy to show how women's lives would be in danger if abortion became illegal again. In an ectopic pregnancy, a fetus begins to develop outside the

---

21   Cheryl's story comes from the Silent No More Awareness Campaign. They can be found on their website: https://www.silentno moreawareness.org/testimonies/index.aspx.

womb, most often in a fallopian tube. This is almost always a non-viable pregnancy, and it carries a high risk of rupture of the tube, which can kill the mother. No physician would refuse to treat a mother in such a circumstance. But doctors and couples who adhere to a "no exception" policy on abortion, and are faithful to the teachings of the Catholic Church, must be careful in choosing their method of treatment.

The United States Conference of Catholic Bishops, in "Ethical and Religious Directives for Catholic Health Care Providers," said Catholics must be careful about the way an ectopic pregnancy is treated because two of the most popular methods cause a direct abortion.

Giving a woman a drug to induce a miscarriage or performing surgery to remove the embryo are considered direct abortions. Another method of treatment for an ectopic pregnancy is the salpingectomy, which removes all of the tube, or just the part where the embryo is attached. Most Catholic theologians say the salpingectomy is morally acceptable because, unlike the first two treatments, the embryo is not directly attacked. Instead, doctors see the tissue of the tube where the embryo is attached as compromised or infected. The infected tube is the object of the treatment and the death of the child is indirect.

A direct abortion is very rarely, if ever, a medical necessity, and it is never morally right. Many mothers who choose abortion for any of the reasons outlined in this chapter will suffer emotional consequences for years and will never forget the choice they made.

If you have previously thought that abortion should be permitted in these difficult cases, I hope I have helped you to think about this tough issue in a new way. There is never a reason to kill an unborn baby.

Now let's move on to another misconception surrounding abortion: that having one is liberating.

7

The Regret of Abortion

Misleading Statistics

Chances are you have come across the statistic that one in four women in the United States will have an abortion in her lifetime. Don't be so quick to believe it. Researchers from the pro-abortion Guttmacher Institute came up with the figure in 2017 to replace the even more exaggerated claim that one in three American women would have an abortion in her lifetime. But by their own description, they estimated abortion rates and estimated the lifetime incidence of abortion. These were estimates with an agenda.

The researchers also failed to adequately take into account the number of women who have multiple abortions—not just two but sometimes four, six, or even ten abortions. A higher percentage of women reporting repeat procedures means there is a smaller percentage of "new" women having abortions. Couple that with the significant decrease in the actual number of abortions, and it seems unlikely that the one in four statistic is anywhere near accurate.

It's in the abortion lobby's best interest to mainstream abortion and make us believe that "everyone is doing it." It's one of the ways they try to normalize the procedure and remove its stigma. If everyone's doing it, it must be okay, right?

But we should ask: Do women leave abortion mills and go on with the rest of their lives without a backward glance? As we will see, that is hardly the case.

Women suffer many physical and psychological complications after abortion. Physical complications from abortion can include uterine perforation or rupture; injuries to the cervix that can lead to premature births in future pregnancies and even miscarriages; pelvic inflammatory disease; the development of autoimmune diseases; sleep disturbances, sepsis, and even death. Psychological effects can include depression, anxiety, alcohol and substance abuse, eating disorders, inability to bond with future children, and suicide.[1]

The Process of an Abortion

To understand how women might feel after having an abortion, we should understand what happens throughout the process.

When she first walks into Planned Parenthood or some other abortion clinic, they take her basic contact information and ask whether she has insurance or Medicaid (in the states that allow Medicaid to pay for abortion) or if she is paying cash. No medical history is taken. If you have ever

---

[1]   Angela Lanfranchi, Ian Gentles, and Elizabeth Ring-Cassidy, *Complications: Abortion's Impact on Women*, (The deVeber Institute for Bioethics and Social Research, 2013).

gone to a doctor as a new patient, there are about six pages of medical history information that you must fill out. In an abortion mill, this is not the case. No such information is ever asked.

Next, the woman is brought into a room to undress where she might be given a pill to calm her down a little. Then, into the procedure room she goes. She meets the abortionist for the first time when she is on the procedure table with her feet in stirrups, ready for him or her to abort the baby. Most of the women don't even know the name of the doctor.

When the abortionist has finished terminating the life of her baby, he or she leaves the room without so much as a word to the mother. Women who have abortions rarely see the abortionist again, unless she returns to that same facility for a future abortion. A clinic worker then brings her to a room where she sits with other women who have just had an abortion, and after about an hour, she is told to get dressed and leave. There is no follow-up appointment with the doctor (as there would be after a normal procedure or operation), no prescription for antibiotics or pain, nothing that you might normally expect if you just had any other kind of medical procedure. It is only in an abortion that good medical practice is ignored.

The Pain of Regret

You might know someone who has had one or more abortions. I personally know thousands of women who have. Over the past three decades, I have been involved in the pro-life movement, and in particular, I have been involved with

Rachel's Vineyard, Hope Alive, and dozens of other abortion recovery programs. These organizations deal directly with women who have had abortions (as well as men who participated in abortions), and it's through this involvement that I became aware of the devastating physical, psychological, and emotional impact of abortion.

Abortion providers like Planned Parenthood, along with pro-abortion organizations like the National Organization for Women and NARAL Pro-choice America, tell women that having an abortion is no big deal. You can have your abortion today and go back to school or work tomorrow. Your problem has been solved.

None of this is true.

A mother who is having trouble dealing with the fact that she terminated the life of her unborn child can discover she has no one in whom to confide. Movies and television shows, the media, and even some politicians promote abortion as a good thing. During a visit to Washington State, the actress Martha Plimpton said she had her "best abortion" in Seattle, and the crowd cheered. When Hollywood actresses brag about their abortion being great, where does that leave the many, many women who regret their lost motherhood?

Women who know their abortion was the worst choice tend to bury those feelings deep down inside. Many women struggle in silence for years, some even for decades.

After one of my recent talks, a woman came up to me and told me of her abortion that happened almost fifty years ago. I was the first person she had confided in—in fifty years! Keep in mind that these women who have aborted their babies have also aborted their motherhood. You don't become a mother when the baby is finally born; you are a mother at the very moment of conception because, as we learned in the previous chapters, that baby is developing rapidly and is not just a clump of cells.

Working with women for many years in the healing-after-abortion programs led me to cofound the Silent No More Awareness Campaign, which I have mentioned in previous chapters. This campaign gives a voice to these women and men who chose abortion and discovered that not only did it fail to solve their problem, as many claimed it would, but instead created countless other problems. Thousands of women and men have joined this campaign to speak publicly about the devastating effects of their abortion experiences. Since 2003, they have been speaking at pro-life events, churches, schools, and—most visibly—at the annual March for Life in Washington, DC, and the Walk for Life West Coast in San Francisco.

"Women who have suffered the loss of their children through abortion are the victims of unspeakable trauma, a hideous unspoken violence," says Dr. Theresa Burke, who co-founded Rachel's Vineyard and has worked with tens of thousands of mothers and fathers, all over the world, who have lost children to abortion.[2]

Yet pro-abortion groups that claim to be the voice of the women in America and who say "listen to the voices of women" refuse to acknowledge the voices of the women from Silent No More. Any woman willing to go public about how fabulous her abortion was finds herself on television

---

[2]   Dr. Burke has said this in several of her public appearances.

talk shows, quoted in newspapers, and celebrated all over social media, while women who tell a very different story, one about pain and loss and suffering, are ignored.

In the pro-life movement, we understand that these courageous women represent the best weapon we have to fight this war to end abortion. Let's hear some of their stories.

Personal Stories[3]

Debbie's story is heartbreaking.

> I was a typical 16-year-old girl. I had a steady boyfriend. I thought I was in love and so did he. I told my boyfriend that I thought I might be pregnant and asked him not to tell anyone. But he told his mom, who then told my mom. This started a huge chain of events. I was called down to the office at school and my mom was there checking me out. I knew she knew just by the way she looked at me. When we got to the car she asked me why I hadn't said anything to her. I told her I was scared and didn't want to know if I really was pregnant. I guess I thought if I didn't acknowledge the pregnancy, I wouldn't have to face it. We went straight to the doctor's office, who happened to be the same doctor who had delivered me. I was tested and yes, I was pregnant, about three months. I remember my mom and the doctor talking about how it was just tissue and we caught it early enough to

---

3   Unless otherwise noted, the testimonials in this section come from the Silent No More Awareness Campaign, https://www.silentno moreawareness.org/testimonies/index.aspx.

have an abortion. I would have to go to the city to get one because I was a little further along but still early enough that it was still just tissue.

I told my boyfriend about the plans for the abortion, and he told his parents. They immediately began making plans for this baby, their first grandchild. His parents said they would set us up and help us get started. I was full of so many different emotions. I didn't know that to do, who to listen to. I told them that I was scheduled to have an abortion. His mom begged me not to. She told me she would adopt the baby and raise the child; that I would never have to even see it. I wanted to believe there was no baby, but just a bunch of tissue inside of me. I knew that didn't feel right. One side of me wanted this baby desperately, and then fear would take over and I wanted to run. I talked to a trusted teacher and she told me what my mother had been saying: "You're too young, it's for the best. You can't miss what you haven't had." Why was this so hard? Why was I already hurting?

The morning of my abortion the baby's father showed up. He gave it one last try to talk me out of it. My mother was afraid I would run off with him so she limited our conversation. I was so confused and so scared. I didn't want to have the abortion, but some of the adults in my life kept telling me that this was the best thing for me to do. That I was too young and having a baby would ruin my life.

The two-hour drive to the clinic was horrible. The closer we got to the city the more I began to feel anxious. I remember wanting to just jump out and run. Once at the clinic I was taken to the back and separated from my mom. I was put in a room with other girls awaiting their turn. One by one we were called. Some girls were crying. I heard my name and I felt like I was in a bubble. I began to cry and shake like I was freezing. I lay down on the examining table. The room was scary to me. I had never been in a room like this. I had never had anything done to me before. The doctor came in and began to get everything ready and the procedure started. I was given nothing for pain. I was totally awake and very aware. The doctor said I would feel some pressure and some suctioning. The machine was so loud. I was moving and the doctor told the nurses to hold me still. I was crying "Please stop, I don't want to do this." It was too late. It felt like my insides were being ripped out. I felt my first real connection with my first child on the abortionist's table. I immediately felt numb, different, and sad.

While in recovery they gave me something for pain and I fell asleep, crying. I woke up hurting and bleeding heavily. My mom was there. I heard girls crying. I started crying. I slept most of the way home. The abortion was never talked about again. It was like it never happened. I began to drift away from my mother. We never went to church any more. The relationship with the baby's father ended. I was deeply sad and depressed and didn't know why. I had no one to talk to about this. The abortion was supposed to fix everything, but

it broke me instead. My body was never the same after
the abortion.

Cynthia Dillard had three abortions as she was studying for
her degrees in clinical psychology.[4] She has no clear memories of the first two abortions; the trauma has blurred her
recall of the events. Ultimately, she married the father of her
two aborted children, but, she said, "That poor marriage, in
a sense, was doomed from the beginning."

When she became pregnant a third time, with a new
partner, she wanted to keep the baby, but her boyfriend
had a different outcome in mind. He wanted her to have
an abortion. "He was psychologically oppressive," Cynthia
said. "Deep down I must have had some awareness of what
I had done the first two times. Like many women who have
had multiple abortions, there is a propensity to keep having
abortions."

And so she had the third.

As she continued her education, she began to experience
anxiety and depression. It became severe enough that she
required treatment. But never in her treatment, nor in her
education anywhere along the way to her doctoral degree,
did the subject of abortion ever come up.

"It never occurred to me, despite extraordinary training
from very learned others, that my depression and anxiety
was in any way related to my abortion. I never thought
about it." And because the academics and the psychology

---

4   Cynthia was interviewed by the author and also shared her story
      with Rachel's Vineyard.

experts almost without fail were saying that abortion had no psychological impact on women, "I touted the party line."

But after her third abortion, things changed. "I began to question my value as a human in relation to God." That spiritual examination led her to the Catholic Church and to a new relationship with a man who also was converting to Catholicism and whom she has since married. A Catholic friend in whom she confided about the abortions urged her to seek healing for her abortions, and although she still didn't believe she had been damaged, she signed up for a Rachel's Vineyard retreat.

"I had a complete about-face at the healing retreat," Cynthia said, "a 180-degree turn." She now knows that her anxiety and depression were the collateral damage of her abortions and that there are millions of women suffering that same trauma.

Here are some short stories that focus on teenagers' abortion experiences.

Marci

The clinic I had my abortion in told me my "fetus" was 7–8 weeks and being only fifteen years old, I didn't know what that meant. Afterward they told me I was actually 10–12 weeks. I got very sick and was vomiting directly after the procedure, the room was spinning and I could barely stand. They pushed me out the door with a plastic bag for my trip home. I had severe pain and hemorrhaging afterward but was too embarrassed to go for help. I suffered with very serious depression and emotional issues for twenty years after.

Shadia

I was fifteen years old when my mother and I returned to Planned Parenthood after the contraceptive they provided months earlier failed. I was told I was eleven weeks pregnant and that my pregnancy was a "clump of cells." I was told to hurry to make an appointment if I wanted an abortion because at twelve weeks, the price would be higher. I was not given any counseling of any kind whatsoever. Today, I deeply regret my abortion.

Sherry

I was 17 years old—the lady at the Planned Parenthood told me I could go to Women's Services clinic in Nebraska to get the procedure. My boyfriend at the time was twenty-three or twenty-four and I was told not to mention that or he would get into trouble. I don't feel like they really had my best interest in mind. From what I understand, they still give young girls the same advice. I was devastated by that abortion and my life spiraled downward for about fifteen years after that. It took me thirty years to even talk about it.

Sue

As a seventeen-year-old teenager I walked into a Planned Parenthood office for relief of the overwhelming shame of being pregnant. I was five feet tall with short dark hair, using my eighteen-year-old friend's ID with her picture; she was 5′6″ with long blonde hair. Guess what? They didn't notice, didn't even question it. I was put in line with the others and escorted out the back door after my abortion. It was only the start of a lifelong regret of the choice I made.

Anne-Marie

I had an abortion at a Planned Parenthood Clinic in Michigan. I was eighteen at the time and eleven weeks pregnant. There was no counseling at all. It was pay at the front desk, then sit in a small waiting room for a few minutes, then into the room where they did the abortions. After the abortion, I was taken to an area with cots and given some orange juice and cookies. When I think back, it astonishes me at the speed with which I was in and out the door. I was not the only one, as the waiting room was full of young women. Planned Parenthood, or should they be named Money Grabbers?

Nicole

They never explained the procedure to me. They never did a pregnancy test. My parents were not informed, and I was fifteen. I was not counseled in any way about the consequences. They served milk, juice, and cookies after the abortion and gave us antibiotics to take home. Bottom line: I was never able to conceive a child again.

Joan

My first abortion was at fourteen in a medical hospital done at just under three months and done by saline solution in the first year abortion became legal in Ohio. I was told by my mother that this was the right thing to do, even though I wanted to go to an unwed home and give the baby up for adoption. After the saline solution was injected into the umbilicus cord, I was left in a hospital room by myself. I delivered a dead baby in the bathroom toilet and cradled it back to the bed with me, then called the nurse. Two years later, while in love in high school, I became pregnant again. My mother and sister took me to a Planned Parenthood clinic. I was given group counseling before the procedure to help alleviate getting pregnant again in the future. When I told them I would abstain, they, everyone in the group, laughed at me and told me I could never do that. I was shamed into thinking the abortion was the only way to handle my behavior. A year later, I was pregnant again and determined to *not* let my mother know. I wed the baby's father and was married for twenty-three years. Abortion doesn't solve the problem. Education on self-esteem, peer pressure, abstinence, and what real love is all about *does* solve the problem of teenage sex leading to abortion. I have spent millions of hours healing from these horrible actions.

Noel

My first abortion experience was when I was fifteen. I went to Planned Parenthood and had no counseling. I was not told correct information about the development of my baby and I felt coerced by the staff members. My second abortion experience was when I was seventeen, and again with Planned Parenthood I had the same experience. By then I was spiritually, mentally, and emotionally damaged further. They were not a help to me. The agency not only helped me kill my unborn children, they helped me kill my own spirit, my psychological health, and my emotional health. This agency harms women and young girls along with killing unborn children.

Emily

I was approximately sixteen years old, pregnant, excited and scared at the same time, in a crisis pregnancy. I went to Planned Parenthood and they instructed me to abort. I can remember clear as day being there. The doctor telling me I'll be terminating tissue/a pregnancy, never once making reference to a baby. Instructing me that this was for my own good. I was approximately six to seven weeks. I remember someone at Planned Parenthood making a comment that if I waited any longer, it would cost more and I'd have to go out of town. This procedure cost $150 cash and changed my life forever for the worst. Planned Parenthood destroys lives.

Tammy

I was a scared sixteen-year-old girl when I had my abortion. It is the worst decision I have ever made and I have regretted it for the nearly twenty years since it happened. I went to a clinic in Illinois. I was a minor, of course, and did not have to have any parental consent. I also did not receive proper counseling. I have no idea to this day what kind of procedure I had. I was also not sure how far along I was in the pregnancy. I do remember discussion between the doctor and nurse stating the pregnancy was farther along than they originally thought. That did not stop them from doing the procedure. I was left afterward feeling worthless, empty, and I regret this experience every single day. It has taken years for me to recover emotionally, although I am not sure if a woman can ever completely recover. It is my hope that women will no longer have abortions and the damage that occurs to women and children will be stopped.

Megan

I was seventeen when I went to Planned Parenthood and was not counseled at all. They told me just about the procedure obscurely but never spoke of the child inside of me as a real baby, just a thing to get rid of. On the day I had the procedure it was never spoken of as even a fetus, just the procedure that would remove the pregnancy. As such I never really comprehended what I was doing or that I would spend the rest of my life burdened by the tremendous guilt of the horrendous act I had done. I wish I could turn back time and have anyone there show me the heartbeat or a sonogram anything to let me fully understand what I was doing. Someone to talk to me about options in a serious non-judgmental manner, to help me reach out to my parents. Now all I can do is stand as a witness that Planned Parenthood, in particular, should not be an option to anyone ever.

Kristine

I was fifteen. It was my first time having sexual intercourse with an eighteen-year-old boy who loved me. I was a high honor student and a gymnast slated for Nationals but I didn't know as much as I should have about sex. That ignorance led to me getting pregnant. I went to two clinics who told me I was too far along for an abortion. There was not a counselor 100 miles from those clinics in Connecticut or the Bronx, as that is where we found ourselves. Not one person counseled me or my college aged-sister and boyfriend regarding all the options. I was from a middle-class family, there was money, and there were options. Not one human being in the Planned Parenthood clinics helped us. We were scared, that's all. But you do not kill a four-month-old fetus, a 4 month-old healthy baby girl who was 100% healthy as shown on the ultrasound – a child of God. I was told to tell my parents. I did. My parents were 100% distraught. Not one person counseled them either. Same story! I was twenty weeks pregnant and perfectly healthy. My parents were advised to abort at the late-term clinic in Boston. We lived just outside of Boston. The abortion killed me, too. That day at Brigham and Women's Hospital, just about a month before my sixteenth birthday, my four-month pregnancy, my child, Allison, was murdered. I died too, and my parents died. So did my boyfriend and his family who were anti-abortion! They loved us kids. We were not homeless children. We had support and financial resources and two middle class homes.

Melissa

I was sixteen when I went to Planned Parenthood. They lied to me. Never confirmed my pregnancy. I was awake during the whole procedure. Saw god-awful instruments on the back of the door. I even asked about the pregnancy counseling center next door; I was told that they were closed. I was visibly shaking, still the abortion was signed off. Never told about my options. Never shown what my baby looked like. You are not offered to see your baby. I was given six pills to take before and an IV during. I was uncomfortable with the man doctor touching me; I wasn't told it was going to be a man. I was told to sit still and be quiet. I was too drugged up to say stop before he started. If one was just "tissue," than others were as well. I can't tell you how many abortions I have had, women lying to women, a convenient "present" that became nothing but an alcoholic blur. I was unable to love my unborn children because I *had* to believe what they told me, that "It was nothing but a tissue." How I hate the women who have destroyed the lives of not only the unborn children but of other women as well, all in the name of "rights." The health issues for me are many due to the ugliness and horror, the weight greater each year in the suppression and then realization of what I have done; the violation of who I was created to be. If anything else, I will be a greater strain on society due to the medical and psychological neglect over the long haul of denial; many like me will be seeking help because they will not know from where the turmoil comes. I need to be heard because I denied myself a voice.

Patricia

My mother made the decision that day for my abortion. They made abortion out to be a solution to our problem and she believed them. I was terrified while in the office of Planned Parenthood and with a frantic plea to not make me go through with the abortion, but it fell upon deaf ears and hardened hearts. They removed me to a room and proceeded to force the abortion on me. No one protected me that day or listened to my cries!

Death from Abortion

As you've read, the emotional and physical problems that follow abortion can last a lifetime. But abortion can also kill mothers. You've read already about Jennifer Morbelli, who died aborting her daughter in the third trimester in 2013. Three other young women died from abortion that year, according to the federal Centers for Disease Control. The organization's annual Abortion Surveillance Report for 2018 lists 396 deaths by legal abortion since 1973. That number might seem small to you, compared to the sixty-two million children who have been killed by abortion, but consider two things: One, abortion deaths are often attributed to other causes, especially if a woman goes to a hospital days or even weeks after her abortion. So the number of women killed by abortion is probably much higher. The other thing to consider is that every one of these women killed by abortion had families who loved them and miss them every day. Alexandra Nunez was a single mother of four in New Jersey who died after an abortion in New York. She told her children she was going to a doctor in Newark to have a cyst removed. They never saw her again.

Tonya Reaves left her one-year-old son with family members when she went to a Planned Parenthood near Chicago for a second-trimester abortion. That boy is growing up without his mother because of that abortion.

The family of Keisha Atkins in New Mexico is still waiting for answers about why the twenty-four-year-old was allowed to suffer for more than nine hours in an abortion mill before she was taken to a hospital. "I'm going to die," were the last words she spoke to her mother.

These were just a small sampling of the many, many abortion stories that are on our Silent No More website, some written by women whom I have met personally. You can read more by visiting www.abortionstories.net or abortion-testimony.com. Every week, more and more women and men share their stories.

You see by these stories that abortion was physically and psychologically damaging to these women. Next time you hear people say abortion is safe and no big deal, please speak up and quote these stories. The voice of experience replaces all the political rhetoric on abortion!

8

A Wider Circle of Victims

The Rights of Fathers

U nborn children are the primary and most tragic victims of abortion, and as we saw in the last chapter, moms, too, are damaged after making the choice to end their child's life. But as much as the media likes to portray abortion as a women's issue, fathers also are impacted by abortion and need healing.

Fathers were left with no rights when abortion was legalized in 1973. Although we do know that many moms are forced into abortion by abusive partners, the law leaves the decision on whether or not to have an abortion up to the mother. Even a man who wants the child and pledges to support the mom and baby can do nothing to stop the death of his child. Imagine how that must feel. By his very nature, a man has the role of being the protector of his child. Losing a child to the violence of abortion can break a father's heart.

Let's hear from some dads who had this experience.

Personal Stories[1]

Kyle was unable to prevent the deaths of both of his unborn children.

In 2007 my ex, Elizabeth, aborted our child after I begged her not to, and even though my pleas were from the heart, it did not matter. She went through with it, despite my pain and sadness.

In 2008 I met Donna, an amazing woman with three kids. We fell in love, and I told her about my ex aborting our child and how deeply it hurt me. She promised me she would never do something like that to me and that she would love to have my baby.

She discovered she was pregnant in March 2009. Donna said she could not have this baby. I was shocked and confused. As I was thinking about our child and all the things I wanted to do with him or her, Donna made an appointment at an abortion clinic. When the day came, I went with her. Once inside, I started to cry and freak out, saying, "I cannot be here, I cannot do this, please, let's leave." We left and I was hopeful that maybe, just maybe, our child would be given a chance to live.

A few days later Donna decided she was going to have a doctor prescribe her a pill that would cause her to miscarry. I begged and pleaded with Donna not to do it. She said she had no choice. I stayed with her

---

[1]   The testimonials in this section come from the Silent No More Awareness Campaign, https://www.silentnomoreawareness.org/testimonies/index.aspx.

through her at-home abortion because I needed to be with our child, even as he or she died.

There is not a day that goes by that I do not think of the kids I lost. I feel as if I am cursed. Why has this happened to me? Both abortions made me feel hopeless, hurt, betrayed, confused, unworthy and unloved. Those are tough things to deal with, and I felt alone.

I do not think people care about the feelings of the man when his child is aborted, especially when he does not want the abortion. Society cares only about the woman, even though it takes two to create a child.

Now, here is Jason, an Air Force veteran who reconnected with a childhood friend after his military service.

Abortion was one of those things I thought would never touch my life. In fact, I really didn't even have an opinion about it. But it came as a big surprise when I had to face the issue personally. First, I was surprised by my response to it, and second, at the profound impact an abortion would have on my life.

When I left the Air Force, I returned to my hometown and got a job in retail. I soon ran into Andrea, a childhood friend whom I hadn't seen in years. She had just moved back from New York and had a five-month-old daughter. Andrea and I started hanging out together and our relationship quickly became sexual. I bonded well with her daughter and before long, we decided to get an apartment together.

I enjoyed family life, so I asked Andrea to marry me, and she agreed. We didn't make much money, but I worked hard to support Andrea and her daughter and was getting frequent promotions at work. Then one day I came home from work and Andrea told me she was pregnant. I was thrilled! Her daughter was almost three years old and now she'd have a baby brother or sister. I told everyone in my family and at work that I was going to be a daddy.

At first Andrea seemed happy about the pregnancy. But after a few weeks, things started to change. She was saying things like, "I'm not sure if we're ready for another child," and, "We can't afford to have a baby right now." I tried to assure her that we'd be fine. Finally, she told me she was considering abortion.

Every time I tried to plead with her to keep our child, she would tell me it wasn't my decision, that it was her body and her choice. I even offered that if she just had the baby, then I would raise it on my own. I became so desperate that I went to a lawyer to see if I could stop her. Unfortunately, he told me there was no legal action I could take. As a father, I had no rights until the child was born. I thought it was ironic that a man could go to jail for not paying child support, but could do nothing to protect his unborn child.

It was on February 25 that my life changed forever. Andrea had gone to the clinic and had the abortion while I was at work. Her sister paid for the procedure and was the one who told me it was done. The last thing I remember after hearing the news was lying in the parking lot of a bar screaming at the top of my lungs. I have no recollection of how I got home or how many days passed before I moved back in with my parents.

Here's another post-abortive father, John, who tried, too late, to stop the abortion.

The day of the abortion was a warm gray day, with a very fine mist falling from the sky. We drove silently to the abortion center, and parked in the lot. She told me to wait in the car, and to be truthful I was relieved not to go into that place.

As I was sitting there alone in my car it began to hit me what was about to happen. How can I sit here and let this happen to my baby—that's my son or daughter they are going to kill! I jumped out of the car and ran into the building. The receptionist told me Janet was in the procedure room and that I could take a seat and wait. I blew past her and after bursting through a few doors came upon a scene that burned into my mind and haunted me for months after.

As I entered that room, Janet screamed out "John, what are you doing?"

The doctor looked at me and smiled, "We are just finishing up, everything went fine." I looked at Janet; she was white as a ghost and crying. Our baby had just been killed! I was unable to stop it. I even paid for it to happen! It was a living nightmare. I stormed out of the building, knocking over some chairs and a trash can in my rage. We drove home in silence, both in shock.

For the next four months I slept very little. I would lie awake at night and stare at the ceiling, reliving that day. When I slept, I would dream of that same horrible scene where I would break into the abortion procedure room, but in these nightmares I would find my dead baby, in pieces. I would wake from this terror filled with rage and grief—how could I let this happen, how could I have been so weak, so evil. But my grief quickly transformed into a seething rage at Janet, the abortionist, and the abortion business that took the life of my child. I was sure that I would never escape this nightmare.

Some men tell their girlfriends or wives the decision is up to them and they will support them in whatever they decide. That is a cowardly response! Most women will take that as a signal that the dad isn't ready, or that he doesn't want to have the baby. Many women have told me that if the dad had welcomed the idea of fatherhood, they would not have chosen abortion.

Paul Marshall found himself at Planned Parenthood looking for parenting classes when he and his high school sweetheart discovered she was pregnant a second time. Their first pregnancy ended in abortion, and this time, they wanted a different outcome.

When my girlfriend and I found ourselves facing a second unplanned pregnancy in high school, we went to

Planned Parenthood to find out about taking classes to prepare ourselves for our new role as parents. We had already lost one child to a brutal second-trimester saline abortion. That decision was made for us by our family and it had a major impact on us both.

But as we know now, Planned Parenthood has nothing to do with helping people plan to be parents. When we asked about taking classes, a clinic staffer told us that was the most foolish thing we could do and that we should have an abortion because in the first trimester, what was growing in her womb was not yet a human being. She showed us diagrams of blobs of tissue and said that's all our child was. Any religious objections we might harbor wouldn't even come into play, she said, because our child was not yet human.

We left that clinic unsure what to do. When she said our baby was not yet human, we believed her. This was new information we had never heard before. A week later, mostly out of fear of what our parents would say about a second pregnancy, we went back to this clinic in Syracuse, N.Y., paid our money up front, and she had the abortion. It took about an hour. Whatever they did to my girlfriend out of my sight, we never talked about. Never. Within a few minutes of walking out the door, I realized we had made a huge, huge mistake. We walked in complete silence until we got to the interstate overpass and then she burst into tears. I can still see the look on her face to this day. And my heart turned as stone cold as the cement of

that overpass. Our relationship ended in bitter hostil-
ity about nine months later.

I was a senior in high school when I found my faith
and began attending church. It was then that I came
to understand how wrong it was to do what we had
done. I became angry and depressed. I dealt with the
pain through massive alcohol consumption.

As we have seen, men who agree with their wives or girlfriends that abortion is the best choice also can suffer regret
down the line. We know from many of the testimonies from
women in these circumstances that they came to regret their
abortion and, in fact, resented the baby's father for supporting them in the abortion decision. What effect does this
have on the men? Let's take a look.

Pat from Ontario, Canada

As a teen I lost my faith. I didn't believe in anything. I
didn't have much money, so when my seventeen-year-
old girlfriend became pregnant I talked to a friend
about it, and he showed me an ad in the newspaper.
She was confused about how to cope with the situation.
We decided to answer the ad and the outcome was the
death of our child. We did it a second time. The same
abortionist preformed a second abortion. While my
girlfriend was on the table he said to her, "So once was
not enough!" My girlfriend had two abortions before
we got married. I never gave it any thought. We only

cared about ourselves. We were self-indulgent and of the world. Eventually, our marriage fell apart.

Eric from New York

I am a Christian, a husband, a father, and I work as a hairdresser in New York City. And I am torn apart by the fact that I did not stop the abortion of my precious daughter.

I began telling everyone, co-workers, clients and friends, how important two days were in my future. The first was January 23, the date my then three-year-old daughter would premier as a Gap model. It was going to be an exciting day to see her bigger-than-life in store windows all over Manhattan. The other was May 7, my daughter Emmanuelle's due date. But before either of those dates arrived, my wife and I went for a sonogram and learned that Emmanuelle had a rare brain anomaly, which would cause seizures and clenched fists. The doctor was very upset that he had to give us the news that our daughter was not perfect. He said, "We'll talk about options tomorrow morning." But we never talked about options.

Instead, on January 15, my wife and I let the doctors kill Emmanuelle. I sat nearby quietly praying while the doctor inserted a huge needle into my wife's belly as she lay sedated, and injected a solution straight into the heart of my precious daughter, killing her instantly. Afterward I thought, how can I ask God to bless me after what I have done?

Chuck from Missouri

I participated in the abortion of my son at Planned Parenthood in St. Louis. I was only seventeen when I learned that my girlfriend was pregnant. We were stunned, and things happened very quickly. I should have been responsible enough to know better, to protect my unborn son and the mother of my child from a horrible, misguided, irreversible choice.

Today I would do anything, give up anything to have that choice back, to have had the courage to say "No!" Instead, I said nothing. I was afraid, timid and complicit by my shame and silence. I'll never forget that cold day. Linda and I rode in her family's Suburban with her mother to Planned Parenthood to destroy our child. The drab clinic was filled with downcast and solemn people, no eye contact, no compassion, and no consultation for the father and grandmother of the baby about to be killed. During the procedure, I felt numb and helpless in that waiting room. We all seemed ashamed and resigned. I felt no freedom of choice and no empowerment. I was required to pay cash for the women's "reproductive healthcare" of aborting my child. The pain of my lost fatherhood remains with me every day.

Effects of Abortion on the Father

Dr. Philip Ney is a Canadian psychiatrist who has researched the effects of abortion on men and women for more than four decades. He shared his insights on men and abortion with me, saying:

> Fathers have been overlooked and underrated for years. The consequence of that is that they don't involve themselves or take responsibility for the family the way they should. Abortion damages a man's self-esteem. They might think, "I am a father. I should be able to look after my child, but I have no legal right to do so." Fathers take their cues from that. If a baby can be aborted without their awareness or consent, it damages their manhood. I think the damage to men is just as severe as the damage to women.
>
> There are men who coerce their partners into having an abortion, threatening to leave if their partner does not agree to abort the child. This is effective because so many women have grown up without fathers. The tragedy, so often, is that she'll abort and he'll leave anyhow. This increasing hostility between the sexes is enjoyed by Planned Parenthood. It's exactly what Satan wanted: Men and women so angry with each other that they won't have children.[2]

Those who study men and abortion, including Rachel's Vineyard cofounder Kevin Burke, LSW,[3] have discovered some common threads in their research:

---

2   Philip Ney, personal conversation with author.
3   LSW stands for "Licensed Social Worker."

- Many men describe abortion as the worst experience of their lives.
- Men experience a variety of emotions after abortion, such as anxiety, grief, depression, powerlessness, guilt, rage, and anger.
- Men tend to defer the abortion decision to their partners (no doubt to avoid the guilt of it being their decision).
- Men may repress their own emotions in an attempt to support their partners.
- Men's relationships may be strained after an abortion.
- Men may experience sexual problems after an abortion experience.
- Men's masculine identity may be threatened by an abortion experience.
- Men experience post-traumatic stress disorder after an abortion experience.

"Whether the father of the baby advocated for or coerced the abortion, was ambivalent or tried to stop the abortion, many experience problems afterward," Burke says. "Abortion attacks the very nature of a man to be the protector of his family. In his role as father, he is entrusted with the care and well-being of his children, and his number one priority is to love and nurture them. Violating this fundamental law of nature can later weaken men in their vocation as husbands, fathers, and leaders."

The Sadness of Grandparents

Losing a grandchild to abortion is an extremely painful experience, but like moms and dads, grandparents don't always understand how badly it will hurt until after it's too late. Just as they had no idea that complete, unconditional love would fill their hearts the first time they set eyes on a new grandson or granddaughter, grandparents of aborted children have no idea how deep the wound would be if that grandson or granddaughter is lost.

Grandparents, like fathers, can play many different roles in an abortion. They may have condoned it, or coerced it, or opposed it. They may not have known about it for days, months, or even years or decades later. But these abortions leave a hole in their hearts, no matter their involvement.

Let's take a look at the experiences of some grandmothers who mourn the loss of their grandchildren.

Nancy Tanner was a dear friend of mine who died in 2020. When she decided to go public about her abortion regret, she knew she had to tell her family, including her mother, Mary Brindle, about the abortion she had twenty years earlier.

Mary, who also has died since sharing this with me, recalled the day Nancy told her about the abortion:

> We were in the car after Nancy picked me up at BWI Airport in Baltimore and we had stopped for lunch. Before we left the car, Nancy told me about the abortion. We just sat in the car and cried. I asked her why she hadn't come to me, and she said she knew what my response would have been. She knew I would try to

talk her out of it. I asked her how she found herself in
that situation and why she thought she had no other
choice. Nancy said that she was thirty-four years old
with two small daughters from her previous marriage
and the father of this baby said it was her choice and
he would pay for the abortion. Nancy felt too ashamed
to confide in me. It was during this conversation that
I realized I had lost a grandchild. That child was my
grandchild. I would have done anything to save that
baby if I had known.[4]

Notice that Nancy felt too embarrassed to tell to her
mother, and the father of her baby did not stand up for his
child. Instead, he paid for the abortion. Nancy was a school
teacher at the time, and her colleagues all told her abortion
was the best solution to this problem. She felt like she had
no other choice. It took Nancy two decades to even talk to
her mom about the abortion, but finally, they were able to
acknowledge this lost child and grandchild.

Betty Fralich shared the story of her daughter Karen's
abortion.

When Karen told me she was pregnant, those were
words I never expected to hear from my teenage
daughter. I wondered, what had I done wrong? But I
saw that we had a problem and we were going to fix
it. I had money saved from my job and I kept Karen
out of school one day and we went off to the abortion
clinic. I'll never forget the sadness I felt as she left the

---

4   Mary Brindle, personal conversation with author.

waiting room. But after it was over, we never talked about it. I totally blacked it out and I told Karen, we don't have to think about it anymore. Karen got pregnant again and got married and had the baby, my granddaughter. Then she had a second abortion in the midst of a divorce but she didn't tell me about it.

Years later I was watching a Christian TV show and they mentioned Karen's abortion. I was the one who took her by the hand and took her to the abortion clinic. I was mainly worried about me and what people were going to think. But after seeing that program, I was transfixed. I didn't know about Karen's nightmares and the alcohol and the suicidal thoughts. I hadn't seen or felt her heartbreak. I sobbed and I mourned the loss of my grandchildren.[5]

As you can see, Betty thought the abortion was a quick fix to her teenage daughter's pregnancy, but she now mourns her grandchild, and both she and Karen speak out so that others will not have to go through what they went through.

Another story concerns Karen Reynoso and her mom, Miriam Kirk.[6] Karen had four abortions within a four-year period, beginning when she was nineteen. Her mother went with her for the first two abortions.

Miriam says, "I was pregnant at sixteen, and I married the father. By twenty-one, I had four children, and by twenty-five, I thought of myself as an old lady. I had given up my

---

[5]   Betty Fralich, personal conversation with author.

[6]   Miriam Kirk and Karen Reynoso, personal conversation with author.

youth and I wanted to save that for Karen. She was a little wild in her ways, and I didn't feel she was equipped to be a mother. Thinking back, I could have stepped up and done something. That's one of my regrets. If we had walked into a pregnancy resource center, I believe the whole story would have changed."

When Karen discovered she was pregnant a second time, Miriam said, "I don't remember feeling a lot of emotion. I took her to the abortion clinic. We knew what the drill was. I remember the third abortion the least, but I do remember the last one, the fourth. I told Karen I couldn't be a party to this anymore. I guess I was starting to realize this was not the right thing to do."

After the last abortion, Karen said she was living dangerously, wanting to die but afraid to kill herself. Soon after, her healing journey began. She started to volunteer at a pregnancy resource center and was required to go through an abortion-recovery program.

"I had no idea all that was left in me," Karen says. "But for the first time, I was able to grieve the loss of my four children." She named the children David, Joseph, Sarah, and Steven (they were the only children she would ever conceive) and held a memorial service at her home that was attended by her whole family.

That memorial service began Miriam's journey in coming to terms with the loss of four grandchildren.

"I didn't fully realize the impact of what had happened, but that was an awakening for me."

Around Christmas, as she looked at the stockings hanging in her home for her other grandchildren, Miriam realized,

"There were no stockings for those four." So she made four stockings for those lost babies. Sewing those stockings "was a time for me to weep and heal and realize the impact of what happened."

She also started volunteering at a pregnancy resource center and began facilitating an abortion-recovery program with Karen.

How poignant that Miriam made those Christmas stockings for her grandchildren lost to abortion. In that very tangible way, she restored dignity to her grandchildren and experienced a deeper level of healing both for her and her daughter.

Now let's take a look at a mother who forced her daughter to have an abortion she didn't want. Here is Kelly Lang's story:

> I was seventeen. I had just graduated from high school and was looking forward to college and my eighteenth birthday. It was a summer to remember—or so I thought—one filled with dreams and hope. But little did I know that soon my life would take a dramatic turn for the worse. For it was later that summer that I had an abortion, an event that devastated me and left me with a bitterness that would haunt me for decades to come.
>
> My memory of that event begins on a hot, muggy June afternoon, as my sister and I were taking a walk around our neighborhood. I shared with her my fear that I might be pregnant and my concerns as to how our mother might react if and when she found out.

Later that day, my sister drove me to a clinic in Wichita for a pregnancy test. My sister warned me to prepare myself for trouble when I finally told my mom.

As my sister had predicted, my mother did not receive the news well—advising me to have an abortion, in part because the love of my life was older than me and I was technically still a minor, being a few weeks shy of eighteen. My mother quickly decided on a course of action. She informed me that I would in fact be going to college, in spite of my pregnancy. She contacted the Wichita clinic and got them to schedule an abortion for me for the next week. She told me that I was not to see my boyfriend until after the procedure was completed. She further informed me that she would drive me to the clinic. After returning home, she would call my boyfriend and tell him to drive to Wichita to bring me home. I was to pay half of the fee and he was to pay the other half. If I did not agree to her demands, she would have him prosecuted for statutory rape.

Over the next few days, my mother spent more time with me than at any other time in my life. Sadly, this was not because she wanted to share my few moments of pregnancy with me. Rather it stemmed from a fear that if I were to spend time with my boyfriend, we would find a way to not have the abortion.

No amount of tears changed my mother's mind. She was determined—and that was that. To make matters worse, as we were leaving town headed for the clinic, I saw the father of my child. The memory of seeing him like that has burned a scar on my heart that still bleeds tears.

The trip to the clinic was filled with pleading and begging. But no amount of pleading touched my mother's heart. Arriving at the clinic, my mother signed the paperwork handed to her. As we waited for my name to be called, I tried one last time to sway her, pleading with her, "Please mom! Please don't do this."

The nightmare continued as my name was called and I was led to a small office halfway down a long hallway. The lady behind the desk asked me if I had any questions. As the last word left her mouth, I was on my feet, running down the hallway, throwing open the double waiting room doors—still pleading and begging for mercy. I fell to my knees sobbing. It was then that I felt my arms being pulled upward and I was dragged to a room where my baby was sucked away.

I lived with the consequences of this nightmare for the next thirty years—constantly waking up to the pain, the void, the anger, the depression, the loneliness, and the self-destructive impulses I experienced every day. I was convinced that everything that ever went wrong in my life was a punishment for having aborted my baby.[7]

More than thirty years elapsed when, after finding healing through a retreat at Rachel's Vineyard, Kelly finally

---

[7]   Kelly's story comes through the Silent No More Awareness Campaign, https://www.silentnomoreawareness.org/testimonies/index .aspx.

confronted her mother about that horrific day. "Her comment to me was that she really didn't remember. It was one of the most traumatic experiences of my life, and my mom said she didn't even remember it."

Kelly and her mom never fully reconciled over the abortion, but Kelly said they came close a few years ago when she was asked to write her abortion story for a magazine. As she wrote, she found herself staring at a purple glass picture frame that she had purchased but never found the right photo for.

"I realized there would never be a picture there. That was where the picture of my child should have been." At Kelly's mother's house, there was also an empty picture frame. A picture of Kelly's son had filled the frame, but he went through a period of self-consciousness and removed his photo.

"That empty frame sat on my shelf in her house for four years," Kelly said. "I came to see that it represented the grandchild she forced me to abort, my daughter, Rachel Charlotte."

Although she has been speaking openly about her abortion for many years, Kelly never spoke about her mother's role in it until after her death.

"She was blind to the truth of abortion, but she was still my mom."

Grandparents can understand that their daughter's abortion was a deeply painful experience for her, but they rarely consider their own personal need to grieve the loss of their grandchild. Still, grandparents, after they grieve and heal, can encourage reconciliation and healing for the entire family.

Siblings Share in the Suffering

When a woman has an abortion, she isn't thinking about the impact of the abortion on children she might already have or have later on in life. But research by Dr. Ney clearly shows that siblings are impacted by their mother's abortion.

Dr. Ney has done extensive work in the area of child abuse and pregnancy loss and has also focused on the phenomenon of the suffering that accompanies the *siblings* of aborted children.[8]

Sibling survivors can feel a sense of emptiness, anxiety, or guilt, and might even have a complicated relationship with their parents as a result of the abortion. They can struggle to understand their value as human beings.

Dr. Ney reflects on this experience: "Observations of psychiatric patients led me to believe that some people were deeply affected by surviving when someone near and dear to them, usually a sibling, died from a pregnancy loss. The symptoms appeared to be most pronounced if the loss was as a result of abortion. Statistically analyzed data showed the most frequent and intense symptom was a feeling they did not deserve to be alive. That was closely correlated to a sense of impending doom, guilt about surviving, pessimism about the future and not trusting caregivers."[9]

---

[8]   If you would like to know about the research of Dr. Philip Ney and Dr. Marie-Peeters, please visit their website www.messengers2 .com for further study.

[9]   Philip Ney, "Post Abortion Survivors," *Messengers 2* (blog), September 19, 2012, http://www.messengers2.com/post-abortion -survivors/.

Now let's hear from some sibling survivors themselves.[10]

Magaly Laguno from Cuba

When I was a teenager, my mother asked me to go with her to an abortion clinic. This was in Cuba where abortion was very, very common, even though abortion on-demand was not legal at that time. I begged my mother not to abort that child. I did everything that I could. I said to her, "I will raise it, Mom!" And I was only a teenager. "I will raise it; I will take care of it for you." She smiled and said, "What would people think?" And I remember sitting in that clinic, inside, and waiting for her to finish and just wondering what more I could've done. I was not a Christian. I didn't really know how bad abortion was. In my heart I felt that it was something bad, but I never really knew until I saw the pictures of an abortion. And I never really knew for many years how much anger I had inside of me against my mother. It took years. We were never close after that.

I attempted suicide shortly after that. And most of my life, I felt that I really had to be the best at everything, because I really had to make it worthwhile that she allowed me to be born. I later found out that she had aborted seven children. And every time we sat at the dinner table, I would think about those who were

---

[10] The following testimonials come from the Silent No More Awareness Campaign, https://www.silentnomoreawareness.org/testimonies/index.aspx.

not there. There's tremendous pain when you're a sibling and your mother aborts. And I'm sure there are many people out there who are feeling this pain.

I got involved in the pro-life movement and I have been in it for over thirty years. And when I first saw the abortion pictures, an internal voice said to me, "That's what your brother looked like when he was aborted." I wrote a letter to my brother I have not met, who I will meet in heaven.

My mother realized what she had done, so many years later, when she saw one of my presentations. It was a great pain for me to have her there. I never told her how bad it was, but she came to one of my presentations and she saw what abortion is. She said, "If only I had known! I love all my children. If only someone had told me. If only I had known." Till the day she died, she regretted her abortions.

Whitney, South Carolina

I grew up in a Christian home with two siblings. I had often told my mom that I wished she would have had more children, because I wanted more siblings. When I was twelve years old, my mom was crying one Mother's Day (as she did every year) and we asked her what was wrong. She told us that she had gotten pregnant as a teenager and when she wouldn't abort, her fiancé skipped town to join the military and her father (my Grandaddy) sent her away to an unwed mother's home, where she was forced to give the baby up for adoption. That was my older brother, John, who we later found and reunited with. So I had my wish, another brother out there for me and I couldn't wait to find him.

But then one night, I had a very remarkable dream. I was twenty-two years old and dreamt I was carrying on a conversation with a woman. This woman looked like she belonged in heaven. She had no wings and was not an angel, but she had a glow about her and I know it sounds cliché, but she was wearing a white robe. She looked to be in her early thirties, had blondish hair, looked quite a lot like my mom and even reminded me of her, too. I had a burning knowledge in the dream that I absolutely had to find out this woman's name, that for some reason her name was of vital importance. This preoccupation may be the reason I don't remember anything of our conversation, but as she turned to leave, I yelled out, "What is your name?" The woman turned around rather slowly and with a somewhat solemn tone said, "Sarah." I remember thinking, "That's it? Why was that so important? It's a very ordinary name."

Weeks passed and the dream stayed with me; it felt much different than any dream I had had before. So one day, as I visited Mom, I began to tell her about this dream. She only half paid attention because she was working on some craft at the time, but I still relayed all the detail and weird nature of the dream. When I told her that I knew somehow that it was so important that I find out the young woman's name, Mom said,

"So, what was her name?" I responded, "Sarah" and my mom gasped and turned pale. Then everything was instantly weird and I knew something was going on. My mother was the most pro-life person I knew, so you can imagine how I felt when she said, "There's something I never told you."

She told me she got pregnant one year after giving my half-brother John up for adoption. Mom said the pain of giving up a baby was so great, that she decided to abort this new child. She said that after the abortion, her parents never spoke of it again and she never shared it with anyone until years later, when she went on a week-long Christian women's conference.

One of the women in her group told Mom she had known many women who had lost their babies through miscarriage or abortion and that it was actually a very healing step to name the baby. She asked if the doctors had told her whether the baby was a boy or a girl and Mom said they had not, but she always somehow knew in her heart that her baby had been a girl. So she thought about it and decided to name her Sarah! My head was exploding and Mom was suddenly very interested in re-hearing all the details of the dream. Mom asked how old Sarah looked and I guessed about thirty-two, and mom told me that is exactly how old she would have been if allowed to live here on Earth. I told Mom Sarah's hair was cut in the same manner her own had been when she was in her early thirties, except that it was noticeably more blonde (Mom and I have medium brown hair). My mom told me that

Sarah's father had naturally blonde hair! I wish I had known when I had the dream that Sarah was my sister. I would have given her such a great big hug.

Now let's hear from a brother.

Nick, North Dakota

When I was twelve years old and in seventh grade, I began praying outside abortion mills, even though at that time I didn't have a clear picture of what abortion truly was or how it affected the people involved. It wasn't until my freshman year that I truly knew what I was doing in front of that clinic.

Three months before I was scheduled to attend the March for Life in D.C., my parents went away for a weekend. But before they should have been home, my brother drove my sister and me to a convent. We were greeted by a priest who told us he would bring us to our parents. We joined my parents in an office and a woman told us we were at a Rachel's Vineyard retreat for women and others who have been hurt by abortion.

My mother then told us she had had two abortions and that she and my father were attending this retreat to help deal with their grief and guilt, and they wanted us to be with them for the final Mass, when prayers were offered up to the babies who were aborted.

Attending that Mass with my family and surrounded by other women who had abortions and truly regretted it gave me valuable perspective and an even better reason to believe what I do about abortion. I was no longer going to the March for Life just for the chance to go to D.C., but because I had people at home and in my family who I had to fight for, not just my mom, but the brother and sister I lost.

Maddie

At a March for Life in D.C. several years ago, a young woman named Maddie, who was then sixteen, read a letter she had written to her three aborted siblings:

Dear John Michael, George Steven, and Mary Elizabeth,

Even though I never had a chance to introduce myself to you as your younger sister, I miss you and love you very much. I'm sorry you never got the chance to experience having Christmas with the family, school dances, being able to see all of God's beautiful creations, and going to church as a family. I wish you were all here today just so I can share memories. Although I haven't had the chance to meet you yet, I'm looking forward to the day I greet you in heaven.

I knew my mother was young, afraid, and confused. At her first abortion she was led to believe that this was the best thing for her to do. Afterwards, she was just left with an overwhelming sadness and emotional distress, which led to drugs, alcohol, and deep depression. During the dark time of my mother's life, she had two more abortions. My mother told me about my siblings when I was fourteen. After church on Mother's Day, my mom took me to the church garden and I sat down on the bench, she put her arm around me, and said, "Madeline, there's something I need to tell you."

She proceeded to tell me about her three abortions and as I looked up at her, I could see her eyes water and knew she was wounded from her past. I did not say much in my response but just a simple, "I love you, you're a wonderful mom, and I forgive you." When reflecting on my mother's story, I feel abortion should be abolished.

I made the decision to become active in the pro-life movement to educate my generation and share the truth about abortion. I stand here today in the honor of you, my siblings John Michael, George Steven, and Mary Elizabeth. For you, I will always be silent no more.

Your Sister,
Maddie

Kelli

Also at the March for Life that year, a woman named Kelli read a letter she wrote to her aborted sister.

Dear Mary Margaret,

I have known about you now for ten years, and I still tear up every time I think of you. You would have celebrated your thirty-ninth birthday this year . . . my little sister. Would you have been the one sibling who would live near me, raising our families together?

Would you have been the one to give my kids the joy of growing up with cousins to share their childhood? I mourn the loss of knowing you, my sister, and also the loss of possible nieces and nephews, a lifelong friendship, and the hole that is at every family gathering without you. Mary Margaret, you are loved and missed.

Your sister,
Kelli

Kelli would also go on to share her story:

My mom was single and already had a five-year-old daughter at age twenty-two. She was embarrassed by another pregnancy and, at the time, thought of the pregnancy as just a clump of cells.

Fast forward twenty-eight years and she felt very different about her baby. She went to post-abortion counseling, told her family, and now knows God's forgiveness.

Knowing I am pro-life, she was worried I would hate her for the abortion, but for me it was confirmation that it isn't something you just "get over." My mom, who defended abortion "choice" for years and buried her feelings of guilt and regret, couldn't live with the secret any longer. She is now pro-life and has spoken about her experience at gatherings in her community.

Frankly, I have been surprised at how much this news hurt and for how long because I would never have expected to miss someone so much who I never even knew. It has made me determined to keep her memory alive, helping others understand how much this is not just one woman's choice, but that it affects so many others for a lifetime.

The testimony of all these sibling survivors reinforces the fact that there is a wider circle of victims impacted by abortion.

Support Pregnant Mothers

Whether you are the mom, dad, grandparents, or sibling losing a baby to abortion, it impacts everyone in the family. It also impacts the aunts and uncles who are missing nieces or nephews. And what about all those cousins you will never get to play with, not to mention all the classmates you will never know? Your life has been impacted by abortion too.

If you consider that we have about one million abortions annually in the United States, that translates into one million families impacted in some way, every year. It is no wonder that we see drug and alcohol abuse on the rise, child abuse continues to increase, marriages are breaking up and ending in divorce, and the breakdown of the family is the inevitable fallout of all this.

You might be put in a position when a friend or family member comes to you and reveals that she is pregnant. You might not realize it, but the very first words out of your mouth are critical. If you say something like, "I will help you no matter what you decide," you have just opened the door to an abortion. If your response is something like, "Wow, I know this is unexpected and overwhelming, but it's also an unexpected blessing," then you are not even suggesting abortion as an option. Memorize this website: www.optionline.org. When you go there, you can enter a ZIP code to find the closest pregnancy resource center to where you live. At these pregnancy resource centers, you can get real assistance for your friend.

I know you have heard the expression that friends shouldn't let friends drive drunk. It's also true that friends should not help friends get an abortion.

Friends might become accomplices to abortion by driving a friend to the abortion mill or helping to pay for the procedure. There have been stories where college roommates have assisted a friend in getting an abortion. In fact, I know at one college, the students in one dorm all chipped in and helped pay for a friend's abortion. They are all responsible for the death of that unborn child!

Friends who are silent about the abortion are also complicit. These friends, too, can suffer from abortion regret.

When family and friends are aware of the abortion decision but fail to help the mother find alternatives, voice their objection, or if they simply express ambivalence or silence in response to her decision, then these reactions can result in the death of that unborn child. The mother then experiences a growing chorus of support, silent or vocal, that confirms for her that an abortion is the only rational decision to her unplanned pregnancy.

You may think that friends don't think about their abortion complicity, but we know from the many people who seek help at healing programs that they are out there, wounded and looking for help.

So remember, never be silent, never be passive, and never be forgetful of that unborn baby. When you hear of someone who is pregnant and in need, reach out and help them find the nearest pregnancy resource center at www.optionline.org.

There are some abortions only you will be able to stop and some lives only you will be able to save!

9

Children Made to Order

Another Abortion Lie

Those who fought to legalize abortion said if women were free to decide whether or not to carry pregnancies to term, there would be no more unwanted children. Women would be in control of their reproductive lives and they could have their careers, delaying marriage and childbirth until they were truly ready. The goal was to make every child a welcomed child, born at a time when the parents felt they were prepared both financially and emotionally to start their family.

In 2002—twenty-nine years after abortion was legalized—the pro-abortion Alan Guttmacher Institute was still optimistic that children's lives would improve. In a report that year, researchers said, "Abortion legalization may have led to an improvement in the average living conditions of children, probably by reducing the numbers of youngsters who would have lived in single-parent families, lived in poverty, received welfare and died as infants."[1]

---

[1] Marianne Bitler and Madeline Zavodny, "Did Abortion Legalization Reduce the Number of Unwanted Children? Evidence from

That turned out to be wishful thinking.

A 2020 report from the Children's Defense Fund, a non-profit child advocacy organization, says:

> For years our country has fallen short of its promise to its children, and as we enter a new decade, the situation for many children is only growing more dire.
>
> One in six children in America lives in poverty, with income inequality having grown to the widest gap our nation has seen in 50 years. Millions of children are homeless and millions more are just one missed paycheck away from losing their homes. Far too many children lack access to quality early childhood care during the most critical years of brain development. For the first time in a decade, the number of children without health coverage is on the rise.[2]

The report also shows that of the nation's seventy-three million children under the age of nineteen, nearly twelve million were living in poverty in 2018. Legal abortion clearly did not solve the problem of poverty.

Another report from the Children's Defense Fund found that 1,844 children are abused or neglected in the United States every day.[3] Legal abortion has not made children—born or unborn—any safer.

Adoption," Guttmacher Institute, January 1, 2003, http://www
.guttmacher.org/pubs/journals/3402502.html.

2   "The State of America's Children 2020," Children's Defense Fund, accessed November 17, 2021, https://www.child
rensdefense.org/policy/resources/soac-2020-introduction/.

3   "A Landmark Law Can Help Keep Children Safely with Their

Seeing Children as a Burden and Punishment

What abortion did change for children is the way we look at them. Think about it. Contraception is sold to women as a great tool for them to control their fertility. And when their contraception fails, abortion allows them to get rid of their unwanted and unplanned pregnancy. This leaves children in a very precarious situation. If they are "welcomed," they are seen as a blessing, a miracle, a tiny bundle of unlimited potential. If they are unwanted, they are nothing but a "blob of tissue," a "product of conception" that can be emptied from the uterus of the mother. In reality, of course, a baby is a baby is a baby, welcomed or otherwise. *But pro-abortion advocates have been conditioned to believe their desire, their choice, is what determines a child's humanity.* The mantra they always proclaim is: "My body, my choice."

For decades after *Roe v. Wade*, the pro-abortion movement continued to insist that a baby in the womb was just a blob of tissue or cells. But when pregnant women began seeing their babies through ultrasound, it became impossible to continue selling that lie to women. In fact, according to the National Institute of Family and Life Advocates, when women considering abortion see their baby on an ultrasound screen, 80 percent choose life.[4]

Families," Children's Defense Fund, accessed November 17, 2021, https://www.childrensdefense.org/policy/resources/soac-2020 -child-welfare/.

4   "Medical Clinic Compliance and Conversion," National Institute of Family and Life Advocates, accessed November 17, 2021, https://nifla.org/medical-clinic-conversion/.

Almost everyone has seen an ultrasound picture of a baby in the womb, often their own or a friend or a relative's. There is no doubt that the figure doing somersaults on the screen, or sucking a thumb, or waving is a human being. The abortion lobby needed a new strategy to counter this "live performance" via ultrasound, so the concept of "reproductive justice" was born. It means the rights of the mother are more important than the rights of the baby, and that only through the availability of abortion on demand can women be equal to men. Perhaps some of you remember the very pro-abortion President Barack Obama saying he wouldn't want his daughters to be "punished with a baby."[5] Abortion has allowed us to see children as a burden, even a punishment, as our former president stated in his own words.

Assisted Reproductive Technology: A Byproduct of Abortion

Legal abortion somehow manages to overlook the fact that a unique human life begins at conception. That is a scientific fact, not a religious argument. A child's human rights also kick in at conception, but pro-abortion groups continue to deny the rights of the child.

Turning conception and childbirth into something we can manipulate played a major role in transforming society. Women are delaying marriage and childbirth for higher

---

5   "Obama's 'punished with a baby' comment sparks protest," *Catholic News Agency*, April 8, 2008, https://www.catholicnewsagency .com/news/12231/obamas-punished-with-a-baby-comment-spar ks-protest.

education and career advancement. But this delay is causing them to sacrifice their most fertile years.

In 2010, the median age for a man's first marriage was 28.2, up from 26.1 in 1990. By 2020, that jumped to 30.2. The median age for a woman's first marriage, meanwhile, was 26.1 years in 2010, up from 23.9 in 1990. By 2020, the median age for first-married women was 28 years old.[6]

Many women are delaying starting their families well into their thirties and forties, and that's where problems can arise. Women's fertility—their ability to conceive a child and carry it to term—begins to decline at thirty-five. Women who encounter difficulties becoming pregnant can turn to what's called assisted reproductive technologies to help them conceive.

The best known of these technologies is in vitro fertilization (IVF). I'm sure you've heard that term, but you might not know what a radical and unnatural procedure it is. Here are the basics.

A man's sperm and a woman's egg are combined in a laboratory dish, where fertilization occurs. The resulting embryo is then transferred to the woman's uterus to implant and develop naturally. Usually, two to four embryos are placed in the woman's uterus at one time to increase the chances of a successful implantation. Please realize that if one of those embryos successfully implants, it means the other two or three embryos—who are already human beings—have died.

---

[6]   "Median Age at First Marriage, 1890 to Present," United States Census Bureau, accessed November 17, 2021, https://www.census.gov/content/dam/Census/library/visualizations/time-series/demo/families-and-households/ms-2.pdf.

A woman undergoing IVF has to have many medical procedures and take hormonal drugs that manipulate her natural menstrual cycle. For several days during each cycle, she will have to give herself injections. It's not easy, emotionally or physically. And it's expensive, about $12,000 per cycle.

Once a woman's eggs are mature, she's ready for egg retrieval. For this procedure, a surgeon inserts a needle into the woman's ovary to remove the fluid from the follicles, which contains the mature eggs. General anesthesia is not required for this part of the procedure, but the woman may be given some sedating medication. Ask any woman who has been through an egg retrieval and she will tell you it hurts.

After this, the woman's eggs are put into a laboratory dish with her husband's (or a donor's) sperm. About eighteen hours later, doctors can tell if the egg or eggs have been fertilized and have begun to grow as embryos. Three to five days later, the embryos are transferred into the woman's uterus via a long, slender tube. Does it hurt? Most women say yes.

After the transfer, a woman must remain in a resting position for an hour or two. Sometimes the table she's lying on is tilted so that her pelvis is higher than her head. She will be given the hormone progesterone for the next two weeks, and then a pregnancy test will be given to see if the embryos have successfully attached to the uterine wall.

In its early days, IVF had a terrible success rate, but that is improving. About 50 percent of women aged thirty-five and under get pregnant through IVF, but that figure drops all the way down to 3.9 percent for women forty-two and older.[7] The shocking numbers of quadruplets and quintuplets conceived through IVF are decreasing as doctors have success implanting fewer embryos, but multiple births are still common.

In using IVF, we are treating our own bodies like incubators and our children like commodities. That attitude towards children and towards life itself explains what can come next in the life of an IVF baby. As you read on, please remember these IVF children were "wanted." Extraordinary means were used and lots of money spent to achieve their conception.

But what if a procedure was too successful? What if there are more children than a couple wants?

Selective Reduction: A Byproduct of Assisted Reproductive Technology

Selective reduction is the next step in this reproductive odyssey. Imagine a couple who has desperately tried to conceive a child, who has invested months, even years, of their time, as well as tens of thousands of dollars, finds the mother carrying two or more babies in her womb. Twins, triplets, quadruplets, or more can be the result. But couples are counseled that they can have the family they want simply by agreeing to kill one or more of the children they worked so hard to conceive.

This procedure is called selective reduction, and it's usually done around twelve to fourteen weeks into the pregnancy.

---

7   "Infertility and In Vitro Fertilization," WebMD, August 1, 2021, https://www.webmd.com/infertility-and-reproduction/guide/in -vitro-fertilization.

You might be wondering how a couple chooses which baby to "reduce." If the woman is pregnant with twins and both babies are healthy, the doctor usually terminates the baby easiest to reach with a needle of potassium chloride, which causes the baby's heart to stop. If the babies are different sexes, then the doctor may ask the couple which child they want to keep, the boy or the girl. You might think this is weird science, but in fact, it is an everyday occurrence in very reputable hospitals around the country.

In a *New York Times Magazine* article, "The Two Minus One Pregnancy,"[8] Jenny, a woman who reduced her twins to a singleton, told her story to journalist Ruth Padawer. "If I had conceived these twins naturally, I wouldn't have reduced this pregnancy, because you feel like if there's a natural order, then you don't want to disturb it. But we created this child in such an artificial manner—in a test tube, choosing an egg donor, having the embryo placed in me—and somehow, making a decision about how many to carry seemed to be just another choice. The pregnancy was all so consumerish to begin with, and this became yet another thing we could control."

Ms. Padawer's eye-opening article also followed a physician as he made his way down the slippery slope of shoddy ethics. As Dr. Robert Evans began doing reductions of large numbers of babies down to twins, he saw the need for the development of ethical guidelines. But by 2004, with

---

[8]   Ruth Padawer, "The Two Minus One Pregnancy," *The New York Times Magazine*, August 10, 2011, http://www.nytimes.com/20 11/08/14/magazine/the-two-minus-one-pregnancy.html?page wanted=all.

improvements in ultrasound technology and IVF successes for older women, he began to advocate for the reduction of twins to singletons. "Ethics," he was quoted in the *New York Times Magazine* article, "evolve with technology."

For many of us, selective reduction is too horrible to contemplate, but it's a reality that couples are choosing. What does it do to them? What are the consequences for parents who go down the IVF road and then choose to kill some of their children? What kind of lasting effect will it have on the surviving baby?

The mothers and fathers may suffer crippling guilt, knowing they deliberately chose to terminate the life of one of their children while keeping the other child. Imagine, at every birthday and special occasion, looking at the chosen child and remembering the child who was killed in that same shared womb (or multiple children in some cases).

Consider this quote from the *New York Times Magazine*:

> A New York woman was certain that she wanted to reduce from twins to a singleton. Her husband yielded because she would be the one carrying the pregnancy and would stay at home to raise them. They came up with a compromise. "I asked not to see any of the ultrasounds," he said. "I didn't want to have that image, the image of two. I didn't want to torture myself. And I didn't go in for the procedure either, because less is more for me." His wife was relieved that her husband remained in the waiting room; she, too, didn't want to deal with his feelings.

The problem is that these couples, like it or not, will have to deal with these feelings.

"Couples who end up playing God with the lives of their unborn children not only violate the moral law; they also violate something fundamental to their identity as parents . . . the protection of their offspring," says Kevin Burke, cofounder of Rachel's Vineyard.[9] "I have discovered in our work with healing after abortions that men, in particular, suffer very profound grief, depression, and anxiety when they participate in reduction decisions and procedures. They may try and distance themselves from the horror to escape the consequences of silencing the natural desire to protect their unborn child. . . . These fathers experience a very traumatic death experience that will leave them and their marriages deeply wounded as they acknowledge their actions were wrong and they deeply regret their decision."

Now consider for a moment the surviving child. Many studies have been conducted about the lives of twins in utero. One study carried out by Italian researchers found that by fourteen weeks, twins in the womb begin making movements directed at their sibling.[10] The babies were seen intentionally touching their twin's eye and mouth regions and were even seen "caressing" the back of their sibling. By the eighteenth week, the researchers calculated that 30 percent of all the babies' movements were directed specifically at their twin. Keep in mind most selective reductions

---

[9]   Kevin Burke, personal conversation with author.
[10]   Lin Edwards, "Twin fetuses learn how to be social in the womb," *Medical Xpress*, October 13, 2010, https://medicalxpress.com/ne ws/206164323-twin-fetuses-social-womb.html.

occur from the fourteenth week and even later when the reduction is using sex selection as a factor. Even if we don't have research yet confirming it, it's reasonable to think the remaining twin is affected by this loss.

There are also psychological effects on siblings of aborted children. Dr. Philip Ney, the Canadian psychologist we have met in previous chapters, tells a story of a woman who came to him for counseling for her six-year-old daughter who was having nightmares, wetting the bed, and suffering from separation anxiety. Dr. Ney, in his interview with the mother, asked her about any pregnancy losses. She told him she had two abortions prior to giving birth to this child.

Then, in a separate interview with the child, Dr. Ney asked her to draw a picture of her family. She was an only child, yet she drew a picture with her mom, dad, a brother, a sister, and herself. She had a sense of her missing siblings.

"What is it like to grow up in a home where you suspect or you know that one of your little unborn siblings was aborted?" Dr. Ney asked. "It creates a whole range of very, very deep conflicts. And we now call that post-abortion survivor syndrome. . . . They (abortion survivors) have in common many of the conflicts that were found in those people who survived the Holocaust. For instance, they have survivor guilt. They feel it is not right for them to be alive. And they wonder why they should be selected when their little siblings were selected to die . . . which is precisely what happened to the people from the Holocaust. Why were they selected to live and some of their friends, relatives, and family were selected to die? And it leaves this deep sense of guilt."[11]

Alternatives to Assisted Reproductive Technologies

I was outraged and heartbroken when I first learned about selective reduction, not only by the immorality of sacrificing human lives to selfishness, but also because I am a mother of twins. My first child was twenty-three months old when I gave birth to fraternal twin girls. Ultrasound was new and not yet used routinely back in the 1980s, so it wasn't until I was starting my ninth month that my twin pregnancy was diagnosed. I clearly remember the panic: how would I take care of twins and my not yet two-year-old daughter?

I understand what these mothers of IVF multiples are feeling, but instead of turning to doctors who are all too ready to kill some of the babies, what they really need is to surround themselves with people who will help them handle this new adventure. In fact, there are support groups for mothers of multiples. I was involved with a group like this, and I am greatly appreciative of their "been there, done that and survived" attitude!

You might hear some people accuse pro-life advocates of being insensitive to couples who struggle to conceive a child when we voice our opposition to assisted reproductive technologies. Doesn't our heart go out to these people? Yes, of course it does. But because of the death of so many embryos and even developing children in the womb, among other moral reasons (like a "playing God" complex), we in

---

[11]   Philip Ney, personal conversation with author.

the pro-life movement oppose IVF and other reproductive technologies.

But when we warn couples off that pathway to parenthood, are we telling them there's no hope they will ever have a family? No! On the contrary, there is a solution that is both morally acceptable and better for the heath of women. It is called NaPro Technology, a healthy and practical way of approaching a woman's problems with infertility.

Through NaPro Technology, a doctor works to identify and solve the problem that's causing the infertility by working with a woman's cycle rather than against it. NaPro Technology addresses the problems of infertility in a natural way that will not result in the death of unborn babies.

Dr. Thomas Hilgers is a clinical professor in the Department of Obstetrics and Gynecology at Creighton University of Medicine in Omaha, Nebraska. He has studied human fertility for a half-century and has been credited with developing NaPro Technology, which began back in the early eighties. There are now hundreds of doctors all over the country using NaPro Technology to treat everything from heavy periods to infertility. One of them is Dr. Anne Nolte of the Gianna Center for Women's Health and Fertility in Manhattan, where women's menstrual problems and fertility struggles are treated as medical problems, as they should be. I told Dr. Nolte that I had heavy periods as a teenager and my doctor put me on the birth control pill. That's the easy way out for doctors, according to Dr. Nolte.

"When the pill came along, doctors no longer needed to look for the 'why,'" she said. "Why do some women have very heavy periods? Why are some women so irregular? The answer now is just to shut down the system with the pill rather than to find out what's going wrong and treat that. We don't do that in any other area of medicine. It is shockingly bad medicine."[12]

Irregularities in the menstrual cycle mean something might be wrong, something is not working the way it's supposed to work. Physicians like Dr. Nolte, who practice their faith even on the job, look for the cause of the problem and work to treat it.

But what about planning one's parenthood?

Two different but similar methods teach women how to monitor their temperatures and to be alert to the body's subtle changes during each monthly cycle.

"Doctors and scientists discovered that the natural family planning chart could also be a diagnostic tool for infertility," Dr. Nolte said. "Like irregular periods, infertility is a symptom of something—hormonal problems, anatomical problems—that are often correctable."

Dr. Nolte said 95 percent of the couples who come to her with difficulty conceiving or suffering recurrent miscarriage have no diagnosis when they arrive, and a majority of them have their problems diagnosed and treated and are able to conceive and carry to term.

"Our success rate is as good as or better than IVF. And we have very low rates of multiple births, and very low rates of birth defects."

---

[12]   Anne Nolte, personal conversation with the author.

There are better alternatives for women that are both beneficial to their health and morally acceptable. To learn more about NaPro Technology, go to www.fertilitycare.org.

Of course, there is another way to avoid getting pregnant when you don't want to be: you simply refrain from having sex. It is to the wonderful virtue of chastity that we will turn next.

10

The Virtue of Chastity

Friends with Benefits

You might have heard the expression "friends with benefits." In case you haven't, it refers to having a friend or friends with whom you also have a sexual relationship.

Likewise, in the media and social media, you might have come across the term "hookup culture." This refers to the troubling trend of people getting together for casual sexual encounters without any kind of emotional attachment.

It's sex for the sake of sex, *and it's dangerous.* No matter how detached we pretend to be to others and ourselves, sex is an intimate act that can leave a person feeling vulnerable, ashamed, or sad. It can also lead to pregnancy. As we learned in previous chapters, contraception is not 100 percent reliable, and there are many physical risks for the young women using the pills, patches, injections, or the other forms we discussed.

An unexpected pregnancy can open the door to abortion. I hope by now you agree that abortion is always bad for the baby, and I think I have made the case that it is also harmful for the baby's mother, father, grandparents, future siblings, and other extended family members.

While every child is a blessing from God, it is true that a teenage pregnancy can alter the course of the lives of both the baby's mother and father. Nothing justifies an abortion, but having a child at such a young age is a tremendous challenge. Sex should not be taken lightly, and not just because it can lead to pregnancy.

Sexually Transmitted Diseases

And there are other reasons for that as well. The rate of sexually transmitted diseases in the United States is at a record high, and according to the CDC, young people between the ages of fifteen and twenty-four accounted for half of the twenty-six million sexually transmitted diseases (STDs) recorded in the United States in 2018.[1] That's thirteen million young people every year infected with diseases that can affect their health and future fertility, or even kill them.

Some STDs that had all but disappeared are now back and sickening millions of people. A headline on a National Public Radio story announced that "Once on the Brink of Eradication, Syphilis is Raging Again."[2]

In 2000, the article notes, "syphilis rates were so low that public health officials believed eradication was on the

---

[1]   "Adolescents and Young Adults," Centers for Disease Control, April 8, 2021, https://www.cdc.gov/std/life-stages-populations/adolescents-youngadults.htm.

[2]   April Dembosky, "Once on the Brink of Eradication, Syphilis is Raging Again," National Public Radio, April 14, 2021, https://www.npr.org/sections/health-shots/2021/04/14/986997576/once-on-the-brink-of-eradication-syphilis-is-raging-again.

horizon. But the rates started creeping up in 2001, grew steadily for the next two decades, then spiked 74% since 2015. There were nearly 130,000 cases nationwide in 2019, according to data released Tuesday by the Centers for Disease Control and Prevention."

Syphilis cases found in newborns increased 291 percent.[3] Newborns with untreated syphilis can experience hearing and vision problems and seizures. The disease also can kill them.

While many types of STDs can be successfully treated with antibiotics, some strains of gonorrhea, another disease that's making a comeback, are becoming resistant to antibiotics.[4] Left untreated, gonorrhea can cause pelvic inflammatory disease in women, which could impact their fertility or increase the risk of ectopic pregnancy.

Some diseases transmitted through sex cannot be cured. Herpes, for instance, is a virus that cannot be treated with antibiotics. Once you have it, you have it for life, and you can transmit it to others even when you are not having an outbreak. The CDC estimates that one in six Americans from fourteen to forty-nine years old is infected with herpes.[5] Many don't even know they have it. And herpes transmitted to a newborn during delivery can be deadly for the baby.

---

3 Tom Hale, "STDs Reach an All-time High in the US for Sixth Year in a Row," *IFL Science*, April 20, 2021, https://www.iflsci ence.com/health-and-medicine/stds-reach-an-alltime-high-in-the -us-for-sixth-year-in-a-row/.

4 Ibid.

5 "Genital Herpes – CDC Fact Sheet," Centers for Disease Control, August 28, 2017, https://www.cdc.gov/std/herpes/stdfact-herpes .htm.

Human papilloma virus is the most common STD in the United States, afflicting forty-three million Americans in 2018.[6] Like herpes, many people don't know they have it. It also can cause certain cancers for both women and men. A vaccine currently on the market is effective against some, but not all, HPV strains.

HIV/AIDS is one of the most serious sexually transmitted diseases. There have been great strides in the treatment and prevention of it since the disease surfaced in the 1980s, but people, including young people, are still being infected with HIV, and the disease is still killing some of its victims. According to the CDC, there were 34,600 new HIV infections in the United States in the year 2018, with 21 percent of them among people from thirteen to twenty-four years old.[7]

Chlamydia is an STD that is particularly harmful for a woman's ability to have children in the future. The CDC rates it as the most commonly reported infectious disease in the United States, with the highest rates in women from fifteen to twenty-four years old.[8] Not only can chlamydia make it hard for a woman to get pregnant, but it also increases the chances of ectopic pregnancy. The prevalence of at-home chemical abortions, which we discussed in an earlier chapter,

---

[6]   "Genital HPV Infection – Fact Sheet," Centers for Disease Control, January 19, 2021, https://www.cdc.gov/std/hpv/stdfact-hpv.htm.

[7]   "HIV and Youth: HIV Incidence," Centers for Disease Control, September 21, 2021, https://www.cdc.gov/hiv/group/age/youth/incidence.html.

[8]   "Chlamydia – CDC Fact Sheet," Centers for Disease Control, July 22, 2021, https://www.cdc.gov/std/chlamydia/stdfact-chlamydia-detailed.htm.

could lead to more deaths among women experiencing ectopic pregnancy as a result of chlamydia.

Having sex with several partners can have disastrous
results for your own personal health. The better option is
to abstain from sex until marriage. Not only is it healthier,
but it is the right thing morally as well. Far from being a
restriction on one's fun, happiness, and freedom, the powerful virtue of chastity and the practice of abstinence can be
liberating and bring profound joy. Let's discuss why.

The Power of Abstinence

Recently, I spoke to Leslee Unruh, president and founder of
Abstinence Clearinghouse, an organization headquartered
in South Dakota whose mission is to promote abstinence
until marriage for men and women. "The Church should be
talking to kids about sexuality," Mrs. Unruh said. "Parents
should be talking to kids about it. It shouldn't be up to the
schools with their Planned Parenthood version that everyone is having sex and that's fine."

Mrs. Unruh is correct that Planned Parenthood has developed sex education programs that are now in use in elemen-
tary, middle, and high schools. The core of these curricula
is that sex is healthy and normal and teens have the right to
do what they want. But an organization that sells contraception and abortion would of course promote promiscuity—it
means more business for them!

Abstinence Clearinghouse, with affiliates in all fifty
states and one hundred countries, was founded in 1996
to distribute resources to those interested in spreading the

chastity message. Among its most successful efforts are the parent-teen events that encourage young people to make a pledge to themselves to remain chaste until marriage.

Purity Balls invite girls twelve through eighteen and their fathers to share a special evening together and to recognize the importance of the father-daughter bond in determining the type of relationships the young women will have with other men throughout their lives. Meanwhile, events called a Knight to Remember are intended for mothers and sons, ages twelve through eighteen, and stress a young man's responsibility to himself and to the young women who will come into his life in the future.

Spending this time together, Mrs. Unruh said, opens the door to understanding and facilitates honest conversations in the future. Both the Purity Ball and Knight to Remember events teach young people that chastity means more than simply abstaining from sex until marriage. Rather, purity is being aware of what types of music they listen to, the movies and television shows they watch, and what they do online.

Let's hear from some people who have attended these events about the impact they had on their lives and relationships.[9]

Hannah

Being pure on my wedding day was so wonderful not only because I was able to step into marriage without the hurt and regret that comes with not saving yourself for your husband, but also because it was another way

---

[9]   These stories were shared with Leslee Unruh and are printed here with her permission.

to glorify God with my life and be a testimony to a broken world that God is not out to ruin people's fun, but that His ways bring true happiness! There is such joy and freedom in marriage when you have no regrets!

The morning of my wedding day I had been dealing with some butterflies and nerves, but the moment I saw Sean that all melted away and I felt calm and so excited that I had the privilege of being his wife and spending the rest of my life with a man who loves me and respects me. He was so worth the wait!

My parents encouraged me from a young age to not try to see how close to "the line" I could get and still stay "pure," but to see just how much I could save for my future husband. I started trying to save as many "firsts" as I could for him, including my first kiss. My very first kiss was on my wedding day with the man I will spend the rest of my life with. It was so incredibly special and so worth the wait!

Melissa

The Purity Ball was amazing! I had no idea so many other girls were remaining abstinent until marriage; it was a real encouragement to me.

Neil

It can be daunting as a dad of a daughter, with no previous experience in this arena, to find a setting where you can talk to her about how valued she is. To talk about the important stuff of life. As I tried to find the tools to make this happen, I always seemed to come up short. Then my wife told me about (and got tickets for) the Purity Ball, a very positive and memorable opportunity for dads to be able to connect on a deep level with their daughters, and to make a lasting memory that ensures that the bond with your daughter gives her a solid foundation for any future relationship. It gives a dad a one-on-one chance to reinforce the value that purity is to be cherished.

Daniel

My greatest enjoyment of the Purity Ball was holding my girl's hands and looking into her eyes while we spoke words of commitment to one another. Abigail was living in that moment and was truly valued that night. There was no distraction; she wasn't focused on other people or what they thought. The honesty of her heart is a healing balm to me. She is her father's joy. My biggest takeaway was witnessing the love of Christ in her eyes. She knows I'm not perfect and loves me anyway. We tore up the dance floor together, and we came home even closer than when we left.

Brett

I've taken all three of my girls to the Purity Ball. When they look back at all the important events in their lives, the Purity Ball is always one they mention.

Kim

The Knight to Remember was a wonderful evening for my son to be uniquely challenged in the area of purity. The event empowered me as a mother to have conversations about sexual integrity, issues of the heart, grace and forgiveness with my son.

Spencer

My parents set an example of what virtue and integrity is through their words and actions. Virtue is something that cannot simply be taught. It is a lifestyle that must be modeled. In observing my parent's relationship, I was shown at a young age the importance of holding the worth and integrity of others at a high regard.

As men, I believe we are called to be providers and protectors. We are called to put the needs of others before our own. Part of that call is being the one to set and respect healthy boundaries in relationships and respecting and honoring women. My dad modeled this in how he treated and interacted with my mom. Being in college, I've learned that the idea of respecting another's purity is countercultural to some people. I am grateful my parents instilled morals and values that impact the way I view relationships. I am also grateful they modeled virtue, helped me develop the skills to recognize virtuous behavior, and disciplined me when I fell short in these areas.

Abstinence Clearinghouse also offers resources for those who want to host events for younger children. The God, Mom & Me Tea gives mothers and daughters ages nine through twelve an opportunity to dress up and focus on the joy of womanhood and the beauty of God's design.

One mom who attended a God, Mom & Me Tea said the event "was instrumental in starting a conversation with my daughter about development and purity. The tea gave me the resources, time and support to make this conversation fun and natural. It also helped her see the ways she is fearfully and wonderfully made by God."

Living Counter Culturally

I want to delve a bit into something Spencer said in one of these testimonies. He pointed out how purity has become countercultural, and he is absolutely right. The media criticize abstinence programs as ineffective and even harmful, while the film and television industry goes out of its way to show teenagers having sex. What you might not realize is that Planned Parenthood has a hand in this too. Since 2016, the nation's number one abortion seller has been working with writers, directors, and others to get abortion on screen as a way to normalize the procedure, and even paint it as heroic. Please be aware that the next show you stream might come with an agenda.

I know many people who waited until marriage to have sex, and almost all of them are happily married with well-adjusted, healthy kids. A 2016 study confirmed what I have always thought to be true: postponing sex until marriage leads to fewer divorces. In a paper titled "Counterintuitive Trends in the Link Between Premarital Sex and Marital Stability," the Institute for Family Studies found that women with zero or one sexual partner before marriage were the least likely to get divorced.[10]

In another study, the same researcher found that people with many sexual partners are "less likely to be married and more likely to be divorced. They're several times as likely as their less adventurous peers to have cheated on a spouse. They also watch more pornography."[11]

Clearly, there are many benefits of remaining chaste until marriage. The good news is that fewer teens are having sex, according, again, to the Institute for Family Studies. Its report on a 2019 study found that less than 40 percent of American high school students have had sex, down 15 percent from 1990.[12]

"Most teens are having less sex and delaying sex longer, and . . . sexually active teens have fewer lifetime sexual partners," the institute reported. "That confirms other data indicating that American teenagers are far more risk averse than

---

10   Nicholas H. Wolfinger, "Counterintuitive Trends in the Link Between Premarital Sex and Marital Stability," Institute for Family Studies, June 6, 2016, https://ifstudies.org/blog/counterintuitive -trends-in-the-link-between-premarital-sex-and-marital-stability.

11   Nicholas H. Wolfinger, "Promiscuous America: Smart, Secular and Somewhat Less Happy," Institute for Family Studies, December 26, 2018, https://ifstudies.org/blog/number-8-in-2018-pro miscuous-america-smart-secular-and-somewhat-less-happy.

12   Charles Fain Lehman, "Fewer American High Schoolers Having Sex Than Ever Before," Institute for Family Studies, September 1, 2020, https://ifstudies.org/blog/fewer-american-high-schoolers -having-sex-than-ever-before.

their parents, challenging the popular media representation of an increasingly sexualized adolescent life."

But what if you have already strayed off the path of chastity? It's not too late to get back on the right road. A group called the Chastity Project offers suggestions for ways to start over. For Catholics, it begins by going to confession.

At the Chastity Project website, Chastity.com, you will find videos about going to confession, as well as testimonials from people who have gone through sexual healing and conversion. Your time will be better spent watching these videos than tuning in to a show produced by Planned Parenthood!

11

Dialogue with the Other Side

Encounters with Pro-Choice Advocates

Hopefully by now, I've shown you why being 100 percent pro-life is the right position to take. Abortion is always bad for the baby, but you have also learned how it is equally bad for the mothers, fathers, grandparents, future siblings, extended family, and, in fact, society as a whole.

Nevertheless, you might have members of your immediate or extended families who consider themselves to be pro-choice. You might also have members of your Church family who claim to be pro-choice. So what should you do? I am not advocating for you to have an all-out war with them over this subject, but when the topic does come up, you don't need to sit in silence either. The most important thing to do when you're in a conversation with someone who thinks legal abortion is a good thing is to stay calm and know your facts (no one wins an argument through dramatic displays of emotion). Pro-abortion people tend to know very little about abortion, so your conversation can be both eye-opening and heartbreaking for them.

Questions to ask a Pro-Choice Person

So let's begin a sort of discussion by first turning the tables on the pro-choice crowd and asking them some questions. The questions below were taken from a pro-life activist training seminar developed by a great pro-life leader and a longtime friend of mine, Mark Crutcher, the founder of Life Dynamics.[1]

- Pro-abortionists say that outlawing abortion would restrict a woman's right to privacy. Is that right absolute? Does somebody's right to privacy exceed another's right to live?

- If what you say is true and the issue isn't really abortion but a woman's right to control her own body, why doesn't your agenda include drugs and prostitution? Aren't laws against those just as restrictive to a woman's right to choose what she will and will not do with her own body as laws against abortion are?

- Why is it that the very people who say the government should stay out of abortion are the same ones who want the government to pay for them?

- Abortion providers say they are in business to help women. Other than offering to kill their children for them, how are they helping?

- Pro-abortionists say the unborn child is part of the mother's body. If that is so, why does it have a completely different genetic code and often a

---

[1]   Life Dynamics website, accessed November 17, 2021, https://life
       dynamics.com/.

different blood type? How do you explain the fact that it has its own immune system?

- If we use the absence of brain waves to determine that a person's life has ended, why shouldn't we use the presence of brain waves to determine that someone's life has begun?

- Since you say that your interest is in protecting women, what is your position on these at home, do-it-yourself, chemical abortions now being offered by many abortion providers?

- We are now seeing the unborn being treated for disease, given blood transfusions, and even operated on. When a doctor does one of these procedures, who is the patient? Obviously, there are two patients!

- Pro-abortionists base a significant part of their argument on the concept of viability. Can you give me a description of what it means for someone to be viable?

- Does it bother you that abortion is legal after the point where medical science has evidence that the unborn child feels pain?

- Why is it that abortion advocates say they want women to have all their options, but they then fight so hard against laws requiring informed consent?

- What rights do you feel a father should have in an abortion decision?

- Why is it that pro-abortionists fight so viciously to keep parents from having a say in whether their minor daughter has an abortion or not?

- If pro-abortionists are mainly concerned with the health and safety of women, why do they fight so hard against requiring abortion facilities to meet the same medical standards as legitimate out-patient surgery clinics?
- If it became absolutely clear to you that the unborn child is a living human being, would you then favor outlawing abortion?
- Should a woman be allowed to have an abortion for absolutely any reason, such as sex selection, selective reduction, or job promotion? If not, what's not a good enough reason to abort?

Sometimes just by making someone talk about their reasons for believing the things they do is enough to convince them that their arguments are weak.

Questions You Might Be Asked by a Pro-Choice Person (and How to Respond)

But you also have to have an arsenal of facts at your fingertips for when they ask you questions. Here are some questions you might be asked and some ways to respond.

If abortion is banned, aren't you concerned that women will die from illegal abortion?

Banning abortion means making it illegal to have one or to perform one. Remember the stories of the women whose abortions we discussed in previous chapters. Many of them said if abortion had been illegal, they would have never considered it an option, but because it was legal, they felt it would be okay. You also learned that abortion was not just a simple procedure, that there are very often physical and psychological problems after an abortion.

Remember what Dr. Bernard Nathanson said about the number of women who died from illegal abortions before *Roe v. Wade.* The number that was reported in just about every news story at the time was that ten thousand women died every year from unsafe, illegal abortion. But as Dr. Nathanson later confessed, he and his colleagues made up that number. The true number was much lower.

Also remember we discussed that women are still dying from "safe and legal" abortion. You learned about Jennifer Morbelli, Tonya Reaves, Keisha Atkins, and others.

So while it is possible that a woman could die in a secret "back-alley" abortion, the frequency with which this happens is much lower than some would have you think. Additionally, it is also true that someone could die (and some have died) from legal abortions. But if we are thinking about the lives that could be lost versus saved, clearly, outlawing abortion would save millions of lives, since so many babies would be given their right to life.

*How can women be equal to men if they are
forced to carry pregnancies to term? Why should
teenage girls be punished with a pregnancy?*

In chapter 9, we discussed how abortion has changed the way we look at children. The culture we're living in now insists that sex is always a good thing and that contraception will ensure no "unwanted" children come from sexual encounters. But if contraception fails, then there's an out: abortion.

At this point, the child in the womb is referred to as nothing more than a clump of cells that can be eliminated. That an unwanted child is something less than human is a lie sold to women at every abortion business in the country. But a baby is a human being with his or her own unique DNA—and rights—from conception on.

Women and girls, of course, are entitled to rights equal to those available to men, but *the fact remains that men and women are different*, and one place that difference cannot be denied, or wished away with nonsensical language, is when it comes to giving birth. Only women can do it.

The journey from conception to birth is miraculous, and it's a gift. Only when we allowed our thinking about the unborn child to become warped could we begin to see pregnancy as something forced on the mother (as opposed to being an honor), and to think of babies as a punishment (rather than a blessing).

Actions have consequences, and from childhood, we are taught that we must live with the consequences of our actions. If you decide to not study for a test, you might fail. If you rob a bank, you might go to prison. If you have sex and conceive a child, though, according to our culture, you can avoid the consequences of your decision to engage in sex by having an abortion. Only when human life is involved are we able to refuse to accept responsibility. That's tragic, isn't it?

If abortion was no longer legal, it's true that some women and girls would have to have babies they might not want.

But there are options after birth, and every one of them is a better choice than abortion. There are "Safe Haven" laws in all fifty states that allow a mother to safely surrender her newborn if she decides she cannot parent the baby. And of course there's adoption, a loving and life-affirming alternative to abortion.

Finally, mothers who choose life for their babies are not punished with lifelong regret, as so many women are who choose abortion.

Abortion is so common, what's the big deal?
Isn't it like having a tooth pulled?

Planned Parenthood and other abortion sellers will tell you that you can have an abortion today and go back to school or work tomorrow. We learned from the stories of the women who had abortions that it was a very painful procedure, and many of them experienced physical problems immediately following their abortion. And all of them, as you know, suffered from regret and often turned to drugs, alcohol, or self-harm to escape their pain. Abortion is not an easy thing to live through, nor is it easy to forget. Even if it was, this wouldn't change the immorality of it. But we should put down the notion that it is a simple procedure. It's not, and the facts show this.

I think life begins at birth.
How can you prove I'm wrong?

At a March for Life in Washington, DC, I once overheard a pro-life college student talking to a pro-abortion student who was declaring in a loud voice that life doesn't begin until birth.

That's nonsense. Since ultrasound first allowed us to see into the womb, it has been clear that the baby is alive and kicking long before his or her birth day. As we discussed in chapter 4, ultrasound makes it hard for abortion supporters to argue that the unborn child is somehow not fully alive. But the evidence for the fact that life begins long before birth can be seen before the first ultrasound appointment.

As I mentioned, a groundbreaking video called "The Biology of Prenatal Development," produced by the Endowment for Human Development and distributed by National Geographic, describes in incredible detail—with images from inside the womb—what takes place from the moment of fertilization until birth. This helps us see that life begins at conception, and not one moment later.

Yet even before modern technology helps us know this with scientific certitude, there is still natural, common-sense knowledge that life would not begin at birth. Mothers since the dawn of time can feel their baby alive and kicking many months before he or she is born.

Shouldn't rape victims have the right to have an abortion?

First of all, women who are raped and choose to have an abortion only account for about 1 percent of all the abortions performed each year. This question is a dodge of the main issue by appealing to a heartbreaking extenuating circumstance. Second, having an abortion after being raped is introducing a second trauma on top of the trauma of the rape. The abortion doesn't erase the rape.

As we discussed earlier, Dr. David Reardon has studied women who have been raped and chose abortion, as well as women who were raped and gave birth to the child. The majority of those who chose abortion deeply regretted their decision, while the women who gave birth to the child said having the baby was a healing moment for them. Some of those women made an adoption plan while others raised the child themselves. So the *voices of experience* have spoken for themselves: Abortion doesn't solve the trauma of being raped. Nor is it fair to punish the baby for the crime of his or her father.

If you're against abortion, don't have one. Why do you have the right to tell others what to do with their bodies?

We have many laws in the United States that tell us what we can and can't do with our bodies. As noted above, prostitution is illegal in most states, as is drug use, and you cannot legally consume alcohol until you are twenty-one, nor ride certain rides at an amusement park until you are a certain height. If these things can be regulated, don't you think it makes sense to make it illegal to kill children in the womb?

I agree late-term abortion is much worse, but isn't that rare?

The Center for Disease Control says that about 1.3 percent of abortions are performed after twenty-one weeks. That might sound like an insignificant number, but it's not. Let's say there are a million abortions every year (we were starting to edge lower than that, but we won't know if the pandemic had an impact on the number of abortions until at least next year). If 1.3 percent of those million abortions took place after twenty-one weeks, that means thirteen thousand babies were killed in the second and third trimester in one year. That's thirty-five a day! Doesn't seem so rare now, does it?

But we should also speak to the first part of this statement. Many people will say they think abortion should be illegal after a certain point. They seem to think once the baby is more developed in the womb, then the abortion is wrong. While this is better than arguing abortion right up to birth is okay, it is still flawed thinking. A child in the womb does not magically become a living human being at some obscure date in the pregnancy. If a mother's third trimester starts on a Tuesday, was the baby not a human being on Monday? What exactly changed overnight? It is important to target these individuals who have a "gut feeling" that abortion is wrong later in a pregnancy. They clearly have something working deep down in their hearts telling them abortion is wrong. They are close to being convinced of the truth and just need a little push from us. If we can convince these individuals, we will tip the scales toward a pro-life world.

Aren't women relieved after having an abortion?

Here again, the stories of women who have had an abortion provide the best answer. Direct your pro-abortion opponent to www.abortiontestimony.com, but also tell them what you have learned. Most of the women did not feel relief, did not feel like their problem was solved. Remember, many of them felt regret immediately, and in fact some of them changed their minds while on the procedure table but were forced to continue with the abortion against their will. Even those who said they did feel some relief immediately afterward later struggled with their choice to abort, with some becoming depressed, dropping out of school, or abusing drugs or alcohol.

What about if a mother's life is in jeopardy? Shouldn't she be allowed to have an abortion?

The sad truth is that the medical profession in the United States is overwhelmingly pro-abortion. To oppose the pro-abortion stance of the American Association of Obstetricians and Gynecologists, a separate organization was formed to speak for those who went into medicine to heal, not to kill. The American Association of Pro-life Obstetricians and Gynecologists believes there is never a reason to pit the mother's health and well-being against that of her unborn child. In fact, they recognize they are treating two patients, so they do everything possible to allow the women to continue the pregnancy for as long as they can. Then they deliver the baby and do everything possible to save the life of that baby. Even now, if a woman has cancer, there are chemotherapy treatments she can have once she has completed her first twelve weeks into the pregnancy. Remember what Dr. Byron Calhoun said: "Just be a good doctor and treat both patients, mother and baby!"

If the baby has a disease or illness like trisomy
18, shouldn't the mother be allowed to abort
rather than having a child who will die?

Through my work, I have met many women and couples
who gave in to pressure to abort their babies who were going
to be born with a life-limiting illness. All of the women and
couples I know regret that decision.

There is a much better choice than abortion in these cases.
You might remember from chapter 6 when we discussed
perinatal hospice. That's an approach to parenting for those
parents who know their child will die soon after birth. The
child is born into the arms of his or her parents and siblings,
and remains surrounded by love until he or she dies. There
is no way to avoid the pain of losing a child this way, but
women and couples who choose to abort have to deal not
only with their broken hearts but the knowledge that they
chose to end their child's life.

One Last Question

A final question you might ask of abortion supporters is: have
you ever seen what an abortion does to an unborn child?

Presumably, they have not. Challenge them to go to www
.LookAtAbortion.org, where they will be able to see diagrams for abortions in the first and second trimester, and
later. These heartbreaking pictures are difficult to look at.
Anyone who sees them will be affected, as the human spirit
has a natural aversion to evil. Often, people support abortion because they simply don't know how gruesome it is.

Putting it before their eyes, while difficult, can be the dose of reality they need to see truth.

I hope these questions and answers have helped you gain the confidence to go out into the world and be 100 percent pro-life, to be able to discuss this issue and defend your position. Remember to start off on the offensive by asking them those questions at the beginning of this chapter. Also, don't be afraid to go back and re-read some of the chapters so you gain a better handle on this issue.

Remember never to be silent and never to be forgetful of the unborn, because there are some abortions only you will be able to stop and some lives only you will be able to save!

Meet the Pro-Life Movement

Preserving Life Together

The pro-life movement is composed of a stunning number and variety of groups both large and small, spanning all ages, professions, creeds, and practically every other designation we can name. Literally thousands of groups are active in the United States alone.

One of the reasons for this wide variety is that the goal of the pro-life movement is so basic and fundamental: *the preservation of life itself.* Because life itself is the foundation to any other rights or traits we have, no matter how diverse they may be, it stands to reason that a cause that seeks to protect the right to life will find adherents across that wide and diverse spectrum of human interests. In this sense, the presence of so many groups is a good and healthy sign.

Another reason for the wide variety of groups is the nature of abortion. It is the intersection of many trends in ethics, medicine, law, psychology, sociology, religion, politics, and numerous other disciplines. Any one of the many dimensions of abortion can easily demand a lifetime of research and labor. I often wonder why some consider a focus on abortion alone to be a "narrow" focus. My experience is just the opposite. The range of intellectual, moral, and practical avenues which this problem opens seem endless. Therefore, there need to be different groups which address different dimensions of abortion: medical groups, post-abortion groups, legal groups, youth groups, activists groups, and so forth.

While preserving and celebrating the diversity and number of pro-life groups, we always seek to foster the unity of the movement and encourage groups to collaborate and combine their strengths wherever and whenever this is practical. We all accomplish more when we work together.

Think of it this way: Each group is just a nice piece of colored glass, but when put together, we can make a beautiful stained glass window. The ways we feel called to join the movement will vary from person to person depending on our circumstances in life. But the important thing is just to get involved, to make a difference. I encourage you to learn more about the individual groups to see if one might speak to you.

As the executive director of Priests for Life, I'd like you to meet my organization first.

Priests for Life

Priests for Life began in 1991 in San Francisco. Father Frank Pavone, who we met earlier in this book, was ordained a priest in 1988, became the national director in 1993, and moved the organization to New York, and in 2017, to

Titusville, Florida. Our core mission is to empower Catholic priests and deacons to be powerful advocates for life.

Over the twenty-nine years of Father Frank's leadership, our mission expanded exponentially as we incorporated other ministries under the Priests for Life banner.

Here's a brief overview:

Deacons for Life – Provides ongoing training to prepare deacons to be as effective as possible in ending abortion.

Missionaries of the Gospel of Life – Invites lay people to take part in a program of prayer, personal study, and pro-life work.

Seminarians for Life – Encourages and equips seminarians to fight abortion and to incorporate into their personal and professional formation for priesthood an awareness of the priority of that mission and the best resources to accomplish it.

Political Responsibility – Engages people to stay educated and involved in the political process at every level of government.

Gospel of Life Ministries – An interdenominational effort to end abortion. It encompasses outreach to clergy, laity, government officials, those hurting from abortion, and all people of good will.

Silent No More Awareness Campaign – A mobilization of mothers, fathers, grandparents, and others who have lost children to abortion and are willing to speak publicly about abortion's impact on their lives and families.

Rachel's Vineyard – Offers weekend retreats for healing after abortion, around the nation and across the globe. Mothers, fathers, grandparents, siblings, and others who have lost a family member to abortion are welcome at the retreats.

Parliamentary Network for Critical Issues – Part of our international work, PNCI works to identify, unite, and strategize with pro-life groups, lawmakers, and religious leaders around the world and at the United Nations to advance respect for life in law and policy.

Stand True – As the youth outreach of Priests for Life, Stand True works to educate, equip, and activate young people to stand up and be a voice for their generation.

Civil Rights for the Unborn – Informs African-Americans and the general public about the harmful impact of abortion and artificial family planning; educates the community about the sanctity of life and activates pro-lifers to combat the harmful impact of abortion.

Hispanic Outreach – An outreach to the Spanish-speaking community, offering all of Priests for Life resources in Spanish.

Priests for Life is one organization among many fighting to end abortion. If you think you would like to get involved, take a look at the various segments of the pro-life movement and see what might be the best fit for you.

Pregnancy Help Movement

The Pregnancy Help Movement began in the late 1960s, even before the Supreme Court decisions of *Roe v. Wade* and *Doe v. Bolton*. Remember that several states had already legalized abortion, so several groups sprang up to assist pregnant women in need. At that time, they were called Crisis Pregnancy Centers, and that name stuck for several decades. They are now called Pregnancy Help Centers.

Let's take a look at the major groups.

Birthright International — www.birthright.org

Birthright was founded in Toronto, Canada in 1968 and has grown to become a pregnancy support service with hundreds of centers throughout Canada, the United States, and Africa. The organization provides confidential support to any woman who is pregnant or thinks she might be pregnant.

Care Net — www.Care-net.org

Founded in 1975, Care Net is a nonprofit organization that empowers women and men considering abortion to choose life for their unborn children. The organization has more than one thousand affiliates and thirty-thousand volunteers ready to provide immediate support to women and couples considering abortion.

Expectant Mother Care — www.emcfrontline.org

Over the past thirty years, Expectant Mother Care has saved more than forty-three thousand innocent children from abortion in New York City, where seventy thousand abortions are performed annually.

Good Counsel Homes — www.GoodCounselHomes.org

Good Counsel is a nationally recognized nonprofit that provides a place to live and community-based services for homeless, expectant, and new mothers and their children. Founded in 1985, Good Counsel now has five homes in New York and New Jersey. The hotline number is 800-723-8331.

Heartbeat International — www.HeartbeatInternational.org

Heartbeat International's worldwide network of more than 2,700 pro-life pregnancy help organizations offer everything from parenting classes to coordinating an adoption plan and providing material aid throughout the pregnancy and beyond.

Heartbeat's hotline service, Option Line, was established in 2003 and has reached more than four million women and men looking for help. Every day, more than one thousand people call 800-712-4357 or go to www.optionline.org for help.

International Life Services — www.InternationalLifeServices.org

International Life Services was founded in 1985 by the late Sister Paula Vandagaer to promote Judeo-Christian values applied to family life, sexuality, and bioethical issues. The organization promotes premarital chastity, the use of Natural Family Planning, and alternatives to abortion.

National Life Center/1st Way Life Centers —
www.nationallifecenter.com

The National Life Center, founded in 1970, is the parent organization for 1st Way pregnancy service centers located throughout the United States. Through its national toll-free hotline, 800-848-LOVE, callers are directly connected to a center near them.

Several Sources Shelters — www.SeveralSources.org

Founder Kathy DiFiore took a pregnant teen into her home in 1981, and since then, more than thirty-four thousand babies and moms have been helped through the efforts of Several Sources Shelters in New Jersey. Pregnant women are offered a place to live while also completing their education and learning job and life skills.

Stanton International — www.StantonInternational.org

Stanton International aims to compete with the abortion industry by establishing help centers next door to abortion businesses. The organization offers pregnancy tests, ultrasounds, client advocacy, and other life-affirming programs to women considering abortion in Idaho, California, and Belfast, Northern Ireland. The Stanton Public Policy Center, an advocacy and educational group, opened in Washington, DC in 2018.

Education

The groups listed here concentrate on educating the public about the humanity of the unborn child and the damage abortion does to women, men, grandparents, future siblings, and society as a whole.

Abortion Changes You — www.abortionchangesyou.com

Abortion Changes You was created by Michaelene Fredenburg as a confidential space for those who are touched by abortion and are looking to begin the process of healing.

Abortion Survivors Network — www.abortionsurvivors.org

The Abortion Survivors Network (ASN) is an advocacy and support group for abortion survivors and their families. It is a leading voice that humanizes the unborn, survivors of abortion, and all impacted by abortion. ASN was founded by saline abortion survivor Melissa Ohden to provide education and outreach to the public about legislative issues that impact survivors, and advocate for survivors and the unborn.

Abstinence Clearinghouse — www.abstinence.net

Abstinence Clearinghouse was founded to provide a single place to find materials in favor of abstinence until marriage. The non-profit educational organization achieves its goal through distribution of age-appropriate, factual, and medically accurate materials, serving agencies and individuals at all levels of government.

American Life League — www.all.org

Cofounded in 1979 by Judie Brown and nine other dedicated pro-life Americans, the American Life League is the oldest grassroots Catholic pro-life education organization in the United States. They are committed to the protection of all innocent human beings from the moment of creation to death.

Anglicans for Life — www.anglicansforlife.org

Anglicans for Life's ministry to help the church uphold the sacredness of life began informally in 1966 and was officially incorporated in 1983, first as the National Organization of Episcopalians for Life Research and Education Foundation and later as Anglicans for Life. The group works to eradicate abortion and euthanasia through ministry, education, pastoral care, and advocacy.

Breast Cancer Prevention Institute — www.bcpinsititute.org

The Breast Cancer Prevention Institute is a non-profit that educates healthcare professionals and the general public through research publications and lectures on the abortion-breast cancer link and ways reduce the incidence of breast cancer.

Campaign Life Coalition — www.campaignlifecoalition.com

Campaign Life Coalition is a national pro-life organization in Canada working at all levels of government to secure full legal protection for all human beings, from the time of conception to natural death. They defend the sanctity of human life against threats posed by abortion, euthanasia, doctor assisted suicide, reproductive and genetic technologies, cloning, infanticide, eugenics, population control, and threats to the family.

Center for Bioethical Reform — www.abortionno.org

The Center for Bioethical Reform (CBR), founded in 1990 as a non-profit educational corporation, works to establish prenatal justice and the right to life for the preborn, the disabled, the infirm, the aged, and all vulnerable peoples through education and the development of innovative educational resources. CBR's projects include the Genocide Awareness Project, the Reproductive "Choice" Campaign, the Corporate Accountability Project, and the Church Project. CBR also publishes educational resources and conducts seminars.

Charismatic Episcopal Church for Life — www.cecforlife.org

The International Communion of the Charismatic Episcopal Church believes that life is precious and that the most defenseless victims of violence deserve protection. CEC for Life seeks to educate and motivate people to understand what it means to believe in the sanctity of human life.

Concerned Women for America — www.concernedwomen.org

Concerned Women for America (CWA) is the nation's largest public policy women's organization, helping members across the country bring biblical principles into all levels of public policy for more than forty years. CWA focuses on seven core issues: family, sanctity of human life, religious liberty, education, sexual exploitation, national sovereignty, and support for Israel.

Focus on the Family — www.fotf.org

Through Christ-centered radio broadcasts, websites, simulcasts, conferences, interactive forums, magazines, books, and counseling, Focus on the Family equips parents, children, and spouses to thrive in an ever-changing society.

Human Life Alliance — www.humanlife.org

Human Life Alliance defends the culture of life and chastity through education, social and political awareness, and life-affirming alternatives to abortion, infanticide, assisted suicide, and euthanasia. The organization has pioneered educational initiatives, worked with policymakers, and helped pregnant women make the choice for life.

Human Life International — www.hli.org

Human Life International (HLI) is a pro-life and pro-family Catholic apostolate at work in one hundred countries on six continents. Since 1972, HLI has carried out more than 1,500 missions to 161 countries, offering pro-life conferences, funding for pregnancy help centers, training for priests and seminarians, and distribution of pro-life resources.

Issues4Life — www.issues4life.org

The Issues4life Foundation works with Black American leaders nationwide to strengthen their stand against abortion on demand and resolve questions surrounding bioethical issues.

Life Issues Institute — www.lifeissues.org

Life Issues Institute works to change hearts and minds through education, utilizing the organization's website, weekly television program (Facing Life Head-On), email news, publications, social networking, urban outreach, and Life Issues daily radio broadcasts.

Life Runners — www.liferunners.org

Life Runners works to impact hearts and minds for saving lives with the "REMEMBER The Unborn" jerseys its members wear while running races all over the country and the world.

March for Life Education and Defense Fund — www.marchforlife.org

March for Life was founded in 1973 following the *Roe v. Wade* decision that legalized abortion. Beginning on January 22, 1974, the organization has organized an annual peaceful protest march in Washington, DC, that annually attracts hundreds of thousands of pro-lifers from all over the country.

National Black Pro-Life Union — www.nationalblackprolifeunion.com

The National Black Pro-Life Union is an organization founded to serve as a clearinghouse to coordinate the flow of communications among all African-American pro-life organizations and individuals.

Parliamentary Network for Critical Issues — www.pncius.org

The Parliamentary Network for Critical Issues (PNCI) is a non-partisan global outreach of Gospel of Life Ministries that works to identify, unite, and strategize with pro-life groups, lawmakers, and religious leaders to advance respect for life in law and policy.

Radiance Foundation — www.theradiancefoundation.org

The Radiance Foundation is a faith-based educational organization that uses life-ad campaigns, multimedia presentations, journalism, and community outreach to affirm that every human life has God-given purpose.

Save the 1 — www.savethe1.com

Save The 1 works to educate pro-life advocates, legislatures, leaders, and clergy on how to articulate a proper defense of children conceived in rape or incest, as well as those with special needs. The organization also offers help and support for mothers who conceive through rape and children conceived by rape.

Silent No More Awareness Campaign —
www.silentnomore.com

The Silent No More Awareness Campaign seeks to expose and heal the secrecy and silence surrounding the emotional and physical pain of abortion. Its goals include reaching out to people hurt by abortion and encouraging them to attend abortion after-care programs, educating the public that abortion is emotionally, physically, and spiritually harmful to women, men, and families, and sharing personal testimonies to help others avoid the pain of abortion.

Sound Wave Images — www.unborn.com

The mission of Sound Wave Images is to provide educational resources on fetal development and facts related to the emotional and physical trauma of abortion. Through the use of ultrasound, the voices of women, men, and families that have been confronted with the truth of abortion are shared.

Stand True — www.standtrue.com

The Youth Outreach of Priests for Life, Stand True is committed to educating, equipping, and activating young people to stand up and be a voice for their generation.

STOPP — www.stopp.org

The organization exists to put Planned Parenthood, the nation's number one abortion seller, out of business. It offers reports on Planned Parenthood as well as provides expert speakers and literature to educate the public about the insidious nature of the abortion industry and its most successful practitioner.

Students for Life of America — www.studentsforlife.com

Students for Life exists to abolish abortion through recruiting, training, and mobilizing youth to abolish abortion. Students for Life reaches young people during the crucial developmental years of middle school, high school, and college, inviting them to join their friends and belong to a movement that respects human life and stands up for those who don't have a voice.

Vida Initiative — www.thevidainitiative.com

Vida Initiative's purpose is to train and mobilize Latino leaders and the people they service to end abortion and build a culture of life in their communities.

Walk for Life West Coast — www.walkforlifewc.com

Walk for Life West Coast was founded in San Francisco to establish a tradition of standing up for life on the nation's West Coast. The annual Walk for Life grows in size each year.

Women's Rights Without Frontiers — www.womensrightswithoutfrontiers.org

This international coalition opposes forced abortion and sexual slavery in China and works to expose the connection between the coercion and human trafficking in Asia.

Legislation

The groups listed here work to create bills, especially on the state level, to limit access to abortion. Laws like women's right to know, parental consent, heartbeat bills, and others were originally drafted by some of these groups.

Americans United for Life — www.aul.org

Americans United for Life (AUL) is a pro-life law firm and advocacy group based in Washington, DC. The group writes model legislation that is available to state legislators as they craft bills in their states. AUL also opposes pro-abortion laws, advocates for or against judicial nominees, and works to defund Planned Parenthood, the nation's largest abortion seller.

National Right to Life Committee — www.nrlc.org

The mission of National Right to Life is to protect and defend the right to life of every innocent human being from the beginning of life to natural death. It works to achieve its mission through education, legislation, and political action. Its activities include providing research, educational materials, information, and leadership training for effective right-to-life citizenship as well as sponsoring legislation to advance the protection of human life and supporting the election of public officials who defend life.

Susan B. Anthony List — www.sba-list.org

The organization aims to end abortion by electing national leaders and advocating for laws that save lives, with a special calling to promote pro-life women leaders.

Legal

The groups below are those we refer to as the legal arm of the pro-life movement. They provide legal representation for individuals or groups that are the subject of criminal or civil charges brought by pro-abortion advocates. They even defend pro-life advocates in cases involving conscience and religious freedom cases. Priests for Life and myself were defended by American Freedom Law Center in a religious freedom case that made it all the way to the Supreme Court!

Abortion on Trial — www.abortionontrial.org

An organization that works to hold abortion providers accountable to existing laws and standards while helping women who have been injured by abortion.

Alliance Defending Freedom — www.adflegal.org

Alliance Defending Freedom is the world's largest legal organization committed to protecting religious freedom, free speech, marriage and family, parental rights, and the sanctity of life. The organization has won thirteen victories at the US Supreme Court since 2011.

American Center for Law and Justice — www.aclj.org

The American Center for Law & Justice is a politically conservative, Christian-based social activist organization headquartered in Washington, DC.

American Freedom Law Center — www.americanfreedomlawcenter.org

American Freedom Law Center is a public interest litigation firm that prosecutes cases to advance and defend religious liberty, freedom of speech, sanctity of life, and traditional family values.

The Justice Foundation — www.thejusticefoundation.org

The Justice Foundation, based in San Antonio, Texas, provides free legal services to clients whose fundamental rights are being violated.

Liberty Counsel — www.lc.org

Liberty Counsel is an international nonprofit litigation, education, and policy organization dedicated to advancing religious freedom and the sanctity of life.

National Institute for Family and Life Advocates — www.nifla.org

Based in Fredericksburg, VA, NIFLA provides legal counsel, training, and education to 1,600 pro-life pregnancy centers.

Thomas More Society — www.thomasmoresociety.org

Through its work on behalf of clients, the Thomas More Society upholds freedom of speech, freedom of religion, and the sanctity of life. Its headquarters is in Chicago.

Activism

The groups listed in this section are involved in reaching people in the public square on the abortion issue. They bring the message of the pro-life movement to the streets to change hearts and minds on the issue and to help women choose life over abortion. All of these groups advocate non-violence.

40 Days for Life — www.40daysforlife.com

40 Days for Life leads forty-day prayer vigils outside abortion businesses twice a year, in the spring and fall. Each vigil is organized locally and ensures a presence outside the abortion facility every day throughout. Started in Texas, the organization now has vigils all over the world.

Bound 4 Life — www.bound4life.com

Bound 4 Life is a grassroots prayer mobilization movement targeting the ending of abortion, the increase of adoptions, and the reform of government and the culture.

Created Equal — www.createdequal.net

Through mobile billboards, abortion victim imagery on jumbotrons, campus outreach, days of action, sidewalk counseling, and more, Created Equal shows and tells the truth about abortion to people who might prefer not to know.

Crossroads — www.crossroadswalk.org

Crossroads conducts annual pro-life pilgrimages across the United States. Each summer, young adults walk on up to three simultaneous pro-life walks across America from Seattle, San Francisco, and Los Angeles to Washington, DC. Walking almost ten thousand miles and through thirty-six states, these young people hope to convert the hearts and minds of others—at the grassroots level—by witnessing to the dignity and sanctity of all human life. Crossroads also conducts pro-life walks across Australia and Canada, made up of volunteers from those countries.

Life Dynamics — www.lifedynamics.com

Life Dynamics is best known for its undercover stings and groundbreaking research on abortion and the industry that capitalizes on it.

Live Action — www.liveaction.org

Through undercover campaigns at abortion businesses, a video series featuring a former abortionist describing common abortion procedures step-by-step, and a news site, Live Action works to tell the public the truth about abortion.

Operation Rescue — www.operationrescue.org

Prior to the passage of federal laws designed to keep pro-life advocates away from abortion facilities' doorways, the organization organized massive protests in many locations, often leading to multiple arrests of pro-life advocates. The organization now acts as an ever-vigilant watchdog, following up and reporting on every instance of a woman harmed or killed by a botched abortion.

Pro-Life Action League — www.prolifeaction.org

Pro-Life Action League trains pro-life advocates to take action against abortion at the local level by building partnerships with churches, engaging the media, working with police, and dealing with counter-protesters.

Pro-Life Action Ministries — www.plam.org

This organization trains sidewalk counselors who, as volunteers, spend time outside abortion facilities to try to reach women heading in for an abortion.

Purple Sash Revolution — www.purplesashrevolution.com

Following the example of pro-life suffragists like Susan B. Anthony and Elizabeth Cady Stanton, women in the campaign don purple sashes emblazoned with the words "Equal Rights for Preborn Women" while calling on lawmakers to pass laws to protect the unborn from abortion.

Sidewalk Advocates for Life —
www.sidewalkadvocates.org

Sidewalk Advocates works to train, equip, and support communities across the United States and the world in sidewalk advocacy, offering life-affirming alternatives to all those present at abortion facilities.

Survivors of the Abortion Holocaust — www.survivors.la

Survivors is a youth-based ministry that exists to empower and equip the rising generation to end the abortion genocide in America. The group has also formed the Society for Ethical Research to confront live dismemberment and born-alive fetal organ harvesting at the University of California, San Francisco.

Abortion Recovery

Listed here are some of the major abortion-recovery programs that provide healing for those wounded by abortion. There was a time when these programs were called post-abortion programs, but it was discovered that the phrase *post-abortion* didn't have any meaning to those who were hurt by abortion and were seeking help. So *abortion-recovery* was adopted as the phrase we now use.

Please note that this is not all the resources for healing after abortion. Many pregnancy help centers include an abortion-recovery program in their centers. Also, there are many Bible study programs available, and many books have been written on this subject.

Rachel's Vineyard — www.RachelsVineyard.org

Rachel's Vineyard was founded in 1995 by Dr. Theresa and Kevin Burke as a weekend retreat program and a safe place to redeem hearts broken by abortion. Rachel's Vineyard has retreats in more than seventy countries, and the program has been translated into twenty-seven languages, with more in development at the writing of this book.

Concepts of Truth International Helpline — www.internationalhelpline.org

Through its international helpline, Concepts of Truth serves as a safe place for people to call if they are experiencing emotional pain after reproductive loss or sexual trauma. The number is 866-482-LIFE (5433).

Entering Canaan/LUMINA — www.EnteringCanaan.com

The Entering Canaan Ministry consists of retreat days, weekend retreats, and monthly gatherings. Entering Canaan accompanies those who are wounded from the pain of abortion to the mercy, forgiveness, and love of God, and addresses the spiritual, psychological, and emotional aspects of abortion.

H3Helpline — www.H3Helpline.org

The H3Helpline is a ministry of New Heart of Texas Ministries. H3Helpline is dedicated to letting those who are hurting from their abortion pain know they are not alone and providing recovery resources. The hotline number is 866-721-7881.

Hope Alive International — www.MtJoyCollege.com

Hope Alive was founded by Dr. Philip Ney, a Canadian psychiatrist in the late 1980s. Hope Alive is a program of intensive counseling for small groups, couples, and individuals. It was designed for those who have been damaged by a combination of childhood mistreatment and pregnancy losses, particularly abortion. The program is now being used in about twenty-seven countries and is rapidly gaining respect among professionals and laymen.

Men and Abortion Network — www.menandabortionnetwork.net

Since 1973, there have been efforts to reach men who have been impacted by the loss of a child to abortion. The efforts did reach some of these men, but oftentimes both awareness and healing programs were primarily focused on women. As a result, millions of men were left without an opportunity to find healing. In addition, the message from the culture was that men shouldn't and don't hurt from the loss of their child due to abortion.

A renewed effort began in 2005, when the first ever Men's Summit specifically addressed the issue of men and abortion. The purpose was to gather key leaders who were involved with the issue of men and abortion loss, and out of that summit, the Men and Abortion Network was created.

SaveOne — www.SaveOne.org

SaveOne offers help for men, women, and family members and friends suffering the impact of abortion. Group, online, and self-study programs are available in this Bible-based curriculum.

S.M.A.R.T Science Matters In Abortion Related Trauma — www.SmartWomensHealthcare.com

S.M.A.R.T. Women's Healthcare was launched in the fall of 2015 by Deborah Tilden. An advocacy training program aims to bridge the gap in the dialogue surrounding abortion by removing labels and neutralizing divisive language.

Silent No More Awareness Campaign – www.SilentNoMore.com

Silent No More Awareness, which I cofounded with Anglicans for Life president Georgette Forney, is a campaign that asks women, men, grandparents, and siblings to make the public aware of the devastation abortion brings. The campaign seeks to expose and heal the secrecy and silence surrounding the emotional, psychological, and physical pain of abortion.

Medical

Many medical associations, like the American Association of Obstetricians and Gynecologists, are adamantly pro-abortion. Pro-life medical groups have formed to help disseminate the truth that abortion is not healthcare.

American Association of Pro-Life Obstetricians and Gynecologists (AAPLOG) — www.aaplog.org

AAPLOG is the largest organization of pro-life obstetricians and gynecologists in the world. Its network of pro-life physicians provides mentoring, support, and communication to all medical professionals.

Sound Choice Pharmaceuticals — www.soundchoice.org

Sound Choice promotes awareness about the widespread use of human fetal material in drug discovery, development, and commercialization, and the rights of every consumer to know what is in their products, including residual human DNA. The organization also conducts research into alternative treatments and products that are ethically acceptable.

This is not every pro-life organization, but I have tried to include the major national groups. Hopefully, you will use this chapter for future study on this issue. It's my wish and desire that this will spark you to get involved in not just fighting abortion but bringing an end to it!

About the Author

Janet A. Morana serves as the Executive Director of Priests for Life and the Co-Founder of the Silent No More Awareness Campaign, the world's largest mobilization of women and men who have lost children to abortion.

Since 1989, Mrs. Morana has held various local and national leadership roles in the pro-life movement. She served on the board of the Staten Island Right to Life Committee. She ran for the New York City Council on the Right-to-Life Line and received the largest percentage of votes of any Right to Life candidate in the Party's history.

She has traveled extensively throughout the country and the world, giving pro-life training seminars for clergy and laity, including at Pontifical universities in Rome, and representing Priests for Life at national and international pro-life conferences. She has helped coordinate relationships between pro-life organizations and the Vatican as well as the White House.

Janet is featured on Fr. Pavone's Defending Life television series on EWTN and is the co-host of The Catholic View for Women also seen on EWTN. She is a weekly guest on EWTN Global Catholic Radio with Teresa Tomeo, has appeared on Fox News Channel and numerous other media outlets. In 2003, she addressed the Pro-Life Caucus of the U.S. House of Representatives on life issues. In 2009 the international Legatus organization bestowed upon her the Cardinal John O'Connor Pro-life Hall of Fame Award.

Janet is the author of the best-selling book, *Recall Abortion*, published by Saint Benedict Press in 2013. Janet's second book, *Shockwaves: Abortion's Wider Circle of Victims*, was released by Catholic Book Publishing Corp. in January 2018.

To arrange a media interview, email media@priestsforlife. org or call 917-697-7039.

To invite Janet to speak in your area, contact our Speakers Bureau at 321-500-1000, ext. 255 or fill out the form at www .PriestsForLife.org/travels or email: travels@priestsforlife.org